Social Foundations
of Education

THE LIBRARY OF EDUCATION

A Project of The Center for Applied Research in Education, Inc.

G. R. Gottschalk, Director

Categories of Coverage

I	II	III
Curriculum and Teaching	Administration, Organization, and Finance	Psychology for Educators

IV	V	VI
History, Philosophy, and Social Foundations	Professional Skills	Educational Institutions

Social Foundations

of Education

EARL E. EDGAR

Professor of Education
The Pennsylvania State University

The Center for Applied Research in Education, Inc.
New York

LIBRARY OF CONGRESS
CATALOG CARD NO.: 65-20311

PRINTED IN THE UNITED STATES OF AMERICA

Foreword

This book discusses the educational enterprise in the United States and the factors which have given and are giving to that enterprise its unique character and configuration. In so doing it deals with issues which have agitated many a society before our own—at least as long ago as the Athenian society which accused Socrates of corrupting the young and condemned him for it.

In our own time and place we seem less concerned about the possibility that the schools are corrupting the young in the sense that it was meant 2500 years ago. Rather, we are concerned with whether and how our educational system can educate the vast numbers of young people of greatly diverse racial and ethnic backgrounds and individual capacities to meet the test of new and unprecedented tasks superimposed on the perennial problems which must be resolved in any society.

There is a reference in this volume to the work of W. T. Harris who, in 1886, spoke of the "science" of education, a study which would be defective if it did not take into account such fields as anthropology, psychology, ethics, philosophy, and the like. Dr. Edgar is not, of course, arguing that education is a science. But he does say that if we are to understand our educational enterprise, we must consider it in a rational manner, i.e., both philosophically and scientifically.

In short, if we are to form useful conclusions about what we should teach, what the teacher should do in the classroom, or what the role of the administrator should be, we must treat the matter as a kind of inquiry. But the process of inquiry implies data-sources of some kind. And in this book we find, in synoptic overview, the relevant fruits of study with respect to economic development, social class, occupational trends, urbanization, the civil rights struggle, the roles of teacher, administrator, and the school treated as a social system. We find here suggestions concerning the task of the schools and some of the significant forces aiding or hindering its performance within a socio-cultural framework which includes the value implications.

The usefulness of the book is not limited, however, to providing a general introduction to an understanding of the educational enterprise as such. Beyond that the perceptive classroom teacher will find much here to reflect upon in guiding the choices which must be made among the range of purposes, subject-matter, and methods of instruction.

Which brings us back to the concern of this book which is, as the author indicates, "the quality of the judgements made and the kind of teacher-education program that will be most effective in improving the individual's ability to make such evaluations." In a similar vein, John Dewey, in his *Experience and Education,* speaks of the need to distinguish between the *cause* of our preference for a particular program or way of doing things and the *reason* why we should prefer it. The cause may lie in mere habit or tradition; the reason, hopefully, is the fruit of inquiry. To quote Dr. Edgar once more, "The ability to take an integrated point of view cannot be developed by a single course, but it represents an important goal for the teacher-education program and—like all such goals—is most likely to be achieved when deliberately sought and planned for." To this end this volume makes an impressive contribution.

CARL TJERANDSEN

Associate Dean
Division of General Education
New York University

Social Foundations of Education

Earl E. Edgar

It is well to remember that the web of professional education has both a warp and a woof. As cloth has both a vertical and a horizontal strand, so education has two interlaced strands, one variable and one constant. The component that varies is one's field of specialization—teaching, administration, school services, and the like. But, however much specialities may vary, there are some constants which every educator should have in his training. These are the "foundations of education," of which Professor Edgar has written so effectively.

Just as every physician must be grounded in anatomy, physiology, and chemistry, or every lawyer in contracts, torts, and criminal law, so everyone engaged in education must be adept in the sociological, psychological, historical, and philosophical aspects of the field. These disciplines are the foundations upon which education rests. Although separate volumes of the Library of Education provide extended expositions of each of these foundations, Professor Edgar's volume gives a synoptic overview of all the fundamentals of education.

It is important to consider the foundations of education as a whole; all too often both laymen and professional educators approach educational problems in a superficial manner. Too often they act on assumptions accepted without examination. Too often they arrive only at ad hoc solutions for their problems. They solve each problem as it comes along, without considering it in relation to other problems. What they need in such cases is a theory that gets down to fundamentals. The word *theory* stems, surprisingly, from the same Greek root which gives us the word *theater,* the root which means *to get a view of things*. Obviously, as one enlarges his view of a problem, theory—far from being impractical—is, in fact, most practical. Consequently, one can hardly commend too emphatically the study of educational foundations.

JOHN S. BRUBACHER
Content Editor

Contents

CHAPTER I

Introduction to Foundations of Education

Foundations and Professionalism

The development of the concept of educational foundations is a significant chapter in the history of education. An essential element in any profession is the development of a basic theory by which professional practice is guided and improved. The dependency of education upon more basic sciences was recognized during the nineteenth century by those who were engaged in building the system of public schools in the United States and establishing programs to prepare teachers for those schools. Some indication of the various disciplines that were suggested as a foundation for the teacher-education program is contained in W. T. Harris' statement (1886) that the "science" of education would be defective if it ignored "nature or mind, or any stage or process of either, especially anthropology, phenomenology, psychology, ethics, rights, aesthetics, religion, or philosophy." Harris believed the "evolution of civilization" to be the key to education, and declared that "no philosophy of education is fundamental until it is based on sociology—not on physiology, not even on psychology, but on sociology."[1]

But acceptance of this concept depended upon the maturation—or, in some cases, the creation—of the foundational disciplines. Out of the natural and moral philosophy of the eighteenth century there grew the many disciplines in the physical, biological, and social sciences. This process of differentiation and change in the spirit and methodology of the study of man and society necessitated a redefinition of the role of philosophy. The creation of new social and psychological sciences brought about, in turn, an increasing recognition of the complexity of the teaching-learning process and the corresponding need for a more adequate theory to guide educational practice. At the same time, the autonomy of the new disciplines,

---

[1] Cited by Merle Borrowman, *The Liberal and Technical in Teacher Education* (New York: Teachers College, Bureau of Publications, Columbia University, 1956), p. 112.

dominated by the interests of scholars rather than by those of practitioners, raised a major problem for the curriculum. The effective integration of knowledge in the foundational areas with educational practice remains a continuing problem in the professional education of teachers.

The identification of the foundational areas and the description of their contribution to education requires recognition of two central characteristics of the educative process. The process is, first, inherently normative, making and presupposing value judgments, for it seeks to change behavior in directions considered desirable. Second, its effectiveness is conditioned by the actual circumstances under which learning takes place. Foundational disciplines are, accordingly, those concerned with the determination of those values which the school should seek to support and foster, and with the identification of those characteristics of the individual and of society that affect the success of the educational enterprise.

Education as normative. The most general definition of the purpose of education is the preparation of the younger generation to become functioning adult members of the society. Whether this purpose is accomplished informally through imitation of—and participation in—adult activities, or formally through schools, it involves the acquisition of certain kinds of knowledge, skills, and attitudes. These reflect, ultimately, the conception of the individual and the social order considered desirable by the adults under whom the educational process is carried on. As John L. Childs remarks:

> Schools always exhibit in their purposes and their programs of study that which the adults of a society have come to prize in their experience and most deeply desire to nurture in their own children.[2]

The education provided by one society differs from that provided by another because of the differences between the values characteristic of the two societies. Nevertheless, even in a given society, differences —if not conflicts—of values may, and often do, exist, necessitating a choice between values. Such conflicts, between or within societies, raise a question concerning the basis for the prevailing value system. Attempts to provide such a basis—not in habit, tradition, or power, but on rational grounds—reveal that education is a branch of morals

---

[2] John L. Childs, *Education and Morals* (New York: Appleton-Century-Crofts, 1950), p. 7.

and social philosophy. Some conception of the "good" life and the "good" society must be invoked, elaborated, and defended. This is the sense in which Dewey defines philosophy as the "general theory of education," in which education is conceived as "the process of forming fundamental dispositions, intellectual and emotional, toward nature and fellow men," and philosophy as "achieving a wisdom which would influence the conduct of life."[3]

Both philosophic and scientific questions are raised in considering the means by which education achieves its purposes. Viewed as means, the methods and materials of teaching and the institutional arrangements for education must be appropriate to the ends. Because the means affect the quality of the values the school seeks to promote, the choice of means is properly a matter of philosophic concern. But the prediction that certain methods, materials, and organizations will produce certain results can be justified only on the basis of an inquiry that conforms to the canons of scientific investigation. It is here that the behavioral sciences are able to make a contribution to the guidance of the educative process.

Education and scientific inquiry. Scientific inquiry into problems of relevance to education came first in the field of psychology. The latter part of the nineteenth century marked the beginning of the empirical study of child development and the learning process, and the development of quantitative techniques for the measurement of ability and achievement. In 1901 Edward L. Thorndike became the first professor of educational psychology at Columbia University's new Teachers College. The appearance in 1913–14 of his three-volume work, *Educational Psychology,* initiated the dominance of psychological foundations in teacher-education programs, and the gradual eclipse of studies growing out of the older social sciences (such as the history of education).

Although the Herbartians had held that a key to both development and learning was the idea that the individual recapitulates (i.e., reflects in his development) the history of the race, this view did not lead to a concern for the influence of present social interaction upon child development and learning. The publication in 1908 of the first two textbooks in social psychology—one by a sociologist and the other by a psychologist—signalized, however, a sys-

---

[3] John Dewey, *Democracy and Education* (New York: The Macmillan Company, 1916), pp. 378, 383.

tematic interest in understanding the influence of other human be-
ings upon the behavior and thought of the individual. The sociologists had emphasized the priority of the group and its influence upon
the development of human nature. Human nature, Cooley wrote,

> . . . is not something existing separately in the individual, but a
> group-nature or primary phase of society. . . . It is the nature which
> is developed and expressed in those simple, face-to-face groups that
> are somewhat alike in all societies; groups of the family, the play-
> ground, and the neighborhood. . . . In these, everywhere, human
> nature comes into existence. Man does not have it at birth; he cannot
> acquire it except through fellowship, and it decays in isolation.[4]

The idea of a self developing through interaction with others was
expressed by Cooley in his concept of a "looking glass self," and by
George Herbert Mead as a process of taking "roles." The notions of
status and role were to become basic components in the explanation
of the sociological determinants of personality. According to these
concepts, society consists of a number of "systems" that denote the
classification of the individual in different ways. Each person, Linton
points out, has a place in the age-sex system and in a system of specialized occupations; he belongs to some family unit and to one or
more association groups. The individual's place in a particular system at a given time is his status; the behavior the culture expects of
the individual in that status constitutes his role. The concept of role,
then, provides a means by which to explain concretely the participation of the individual in his culture, for that participation is determined by the "particular cultural demands which his society makes
upon him because of his place in it."[5]

Representatives of a number of disciplines (anthropology in particular) contributed to the development of the concept of culture.
The concept was first defined by Tylor, in 1871, as "that complex
whole which includes knowledge, belief, art, law, morals, custom,
and any other capabilities and habits acquired by man as a member
of society."[6] As Gabriel points out, anthropological study was stimulated in the United States during the nineteenth century by the

---

[4] Charles H. Cooley, *Social Organization* (New York: Charles Scribner's Sons, 1909), p. 29.
[5] Ralph Linton, *The Cultural Background of Personality* (New York: Appleton-Century-Crofts, 1945), pp. 55, 61–62, 76–82.
[6] A. L. Kroeber and Clyde Kluckhohn, *Culture: A Critical Review of Concepts and Definitions* (New York: Random House, 1963), pp. 81, 284, 292.

presence of Indian tribes on the frontier, which served constantly to remind at least some Americans that "human society took other forms than those which they were pleased to call civilization."[7] From time to time there appeared descriptions of Indian society and folklore; among them was Lewis B. Morgan's study of the Iroquois, which was followed in 1878 by his pioneer work in cultural anthropology, *Ancient Society*. In 1913 Boas published *The Mind of Primitive Man*. Twenty years later Benedict stressed the importance of studying a wide selection of historically unrelated societies. These societies were to serve as "laboratories" in which to trace the difference between what is original in human nature and what is learned. The lesson of such studies was that

> The life history of the individual is first and foremost an accommodation to the patterns and standards traditionally handed down in his community. From the moment of his birth, the customs into which he is born shape his experience and behavior. By the time he can talk, he is the little creature of his culture; and by the time he is grown and able to take part in its activities, its habits are his habits, its beliefs his beliefs, its impossibilities his impossibilities. Every child that is born into his group will share them with him, and no child born into one on the opposite side of the globe can ever achieve the thousandth part.[8]

The description of the individual as the *creature of his culture* perhaps exaggerated the importance of culture as much as eighteenth-century political and economic theory had exaggerated the self-sufficiency of the individual. The result, however, was a focusing of attention upon the fact that human nature is in part learned, and upon the processes—and agencies—through which the learning takes place. Some of the problems of the school (as one of the agencies of socialization) could be viewed in a new and more comprehensive light. It was recognized that the principles gained from the study of acculturation are as pertinent to the understanding of the teaching-learning process as are studies of perception or retention.[9]

---

[7] Ralph Henry Gabriel, *The Course of American Democratic Thought,* 2nd ed. (New York: The Ronald Press Company, 1956), p. 172. Copyright © by the Ronald Press Company.

[8] Ruth Benedict, *Patterns of Culture* (New York: New American Library of World Literature, 1934), p. 2. Reprinted by permission of Houghton Mifflin Company, New York.

[9] See Bernard J. Siegel, "Models for the Analysis of the Educative Process in American Communities," in *Education and Anthropology,* edited by George Spindler (Stanford: Stanford University Press, 1955), pp. 41ff.

If learning is reinforced by the experience of success, the fact that success is culturally defined becomes relevant to the methods and materials with which the school promotes learning. The concept of the school as a part of culture, and of culture as a pattern or configuration, suggests the necessity (if the work of the school is to be completely understood) of investigating the total culture, including its values, as the context within which the school functions.

The Foundations of Education in the Teacher-Education Program

The Columbia University Program. The first formal program in the foundations of education was established in 1934 by Columbia University's Teachers College. Its origin, however, may be ascribed to the concept of the progressive role of the school in society —a concept formulated in Lester Ward's *Dynamic Sociology* (1883) and accepted by John Dewey as the basic principle of his educational philosophy. Brim has called Dewey's *School and Society* (1899) the "first work to present a systematic institutional treatment of education."[10] The publication of Dewey's *Democracy and Education* (1916) further stimulated both the sociological interest in schools and the demand for their democratization. The democratic slogans of World War I provided a basis upon which educators could renew their call for the greater participation of teachers in the making of educational policy in American schools. This participation, in turn, required that the teacher-education program provide the opportunity for prospective teachers to gain an understanding of social forces and their impact upon the schools.

During the 1920's, the men who were to establish the Division of Foundations at Columbia University formed a discussion group. This group, under the chairmanship of William Heard Kilpatrick, was to make an intensive study of all the foundations of education. It formed the nucleus of the sixty Fellows of the John Dewey Society for the Study of Education and Culture, and contributed to the interpretation of society and the school expressed in the journal, *The Social Frontier,* and in *The Educational Frontier* (1933). In

---

[10] Orville G. Brim, Jr., *Sociology and the Field of Education* (New York: Russell Sage Foundation, 1958), p. 9.

the latter volume, a chapter produced jointly by Dewey and Childs expressed the conviction that

> ... any educational philosophy which is to be significant for American education at the present time must be the expression of a social philosophy and that the social and educational theories and conceptions must be developed with definite reference to the needs and issues which mark and divide our domestic, economic, and political life in the generation of which we are a part.[11]

The "widespread demand for drastic curtailment of educational services" because of the depression of the 1930's, they wrote, showed

> ... that educators as educators need to become acquainted with the workings of our industrial and financial system; to discover what is wrong and why; and to be interested from the standpoint of their own calling in methods of social action that will improve conditions.[12]

This requirement, furthermore, applied as well to "times when economic forces are working inequitably even when there is no marked depression," to "conditions which affect the life of children and youth out of schools" as well as "conditions which present themselves in the school."[13]

Such convictions were an important influence in the establishment of the Columbia Foundations Program. That program was also the professional-school counterpart of the general education movement in undergraduate curricula that was gaining momentum at the time and in which Columbia played a leading part. Just as the key word in general education was *integration,* so the key concept in the Foundations movement was to "see society as a *whole* and see education as a *total enterprise* in relation to the society and culture."[14] In administrative terms, this led to the organization of a Division of Foundations of Education that brought together the many specialized courses making up the Teachers College graduate program into two departments: Psychological Foundations, and Social and Philosophical Foundations. It also led to the creation of

---

[11] William H. Kilpatrick (ed.), *The Educational Frontier* (New York: Appleton-Century-Crofts, 1933), pp. 35–36.

[12] *Ibid.,* p. 37.

[13] *Ibid.*

[14] R. Freeman Butts, in a letter to W. H. Cowley, reprinted in Charles J. Brauner, *American Educational Theory* (Englewood Cliffs, N.J.: Prentice-Hall, Inc., 1964), pp. 202–204.

an integrated course, Education in American Culture, required of
all candidates for the master's degree.

Aims and goals.   In the introduction to the source materials
used in this course, two major theses were set forth as the basis for
understanding the work of the schools: the school is a social institution; and it constitutes a form of social action. The first principle
meant that organized education is never "conducted with sole reference to absolute and universal principles," but inevitably "reflects
in varying proportion the experience, the conditions, the hopes,
fears, and ideals of a particular people or cultural group at a particular point in history." Therefore

> . . . any individual being prepared to discharge intelligently the
> task of shaping educational theory or practice should begin with an
> examination in historical and geographical perspective of the so-
> ciety to be served—its essential traditions, its great cultural pat-
> terns, its relations with other societies, its basic resources and po-
> tentialities, its controlling ideals, values, and interests.[15]

But more is involved in the task of formulating educational policies
and programs than the gathering of data about society and culture.
Facts must be "selected, interpreted, and woven into patterns of
utility and purpose." This followed from the second thesis:

> Always and everywhere organized education is a form of prac-
> tical endeavor—a form of social action. It is a program, deliberately
> conceived by some society or group, to achieve certain purposes.
> This means that the educator fails in his line of duty if he refuses
> to look beyond the walls of academy and laboratory, reject the ir-
> responsible role of disinterested spectator, make ethical and aes-
> thetic choices, and operate under the guidance of some recognized
> conception of social welfare and policy.[16]

In attempting to combine the objective study of society with a
concern for the development of a commitment to "some recognized
conception of social welfare," educational foundations inherited the
dispute between educational sociology and the sociology of education. These labels represented the difference between those who
considered the sociological study of education a part of the "science"

---

[15] Harold Rugg (ed.), *Readings in the Foundations of Education* (New York:
Teachers College, Bureau of Publications, Columbia University, 1941), Vol. I,
pp. ix–x.
[16] *Ibid.,* pp. x–xi.

of education and those who regarded it as a branch of sociology.[17] The tensions between the two viewpoints are revealed in the criticisms directed by partisans of the sociology of education against educational sociology. Wilbur B. Brookover, for example, has described courses in educational sociology as a "hodgepodge of subjects which instructors in sociology and education had put together for the training of teachers and others interested in education," a hodgepodge that "competent sociologists could not continue to respect," particularly in view of the emphasis such courses placed on "value judgments, educational technology, and other materials foreign to the scientific analysis of social interaction." He called for a sociology of education that would be a "scientific analysis of the social processes and social patterns involved in the educational system."[18] Neal Gross has criticized the research literature in the sociological analysis of education for its "undue emphasis upon description in contrast to analysis," its lack of theoretical orientation, and its failure to yield "hypotheses of sociological importance" and to meet "the methodological standards generally accepted as minimal criteria for competent research inquiries." An additional reason that sociological analysis of education is "a relatively underdeveloped and unfashionable subfield of sociology," according to Gross, has been its association with schools and departments of education, which are "at or near the bottom of the academic prestige hierarchy."[19]

Educational policy.   Charles J. Brauner has criticized the Columbia and Illinois Foundations programs on the ground that both tend to sacrifice scholarship for the sake of subjective commitment, so that "foundational courses resemble a minister's sermons rather than a professor's lectures."[20] A concern for the absence of scholarship in the various foundational courses in psychology, philosophy, and sociology pervades Conant's discussion of the foundational

---

[17] Blaine W. Mercer and Edwin R. Carr, *Education and the Social Order* (New York: Holt, Rinehart & Winston, Inc., 1957), pp. 3–6.

[18] Wilbur B. Brookover, *A Sociology of Education* (New York: American Book Company, 1955), pp. 23, 28, 31. (A second edition of this title, by Brookover and Gottlieb, was published in 1964.)

[19] Neal Gross, "The Sociology of Education," in *Sociology Today,* edited by Robert K. Merton, Leonard Broom, and Leonard S. Cottrell, Jr. (New York: Basic Books, Inc., 1959), pp. 128–52; see also Brim, *op. cit.,* pp. 9–11.

[20] Brauner, *op. cit.,* p. 220.

phase of the teacher-education program.[21] Borrowman's more sympathetic account compares those handling the foundational materials with the "peacemakers who find themselves turned upon by both parties to a dispute which they attempt to mediate." He refers to the fact that foundations courses are considered too scholarly and intellectual by practitioners, and too practice-centered and unscholarly by representatives of the academic disciplines.[22]

The problem of maintaining ties between foundations courses and scholarship—a problem shared by the general education movement—becomes even more critical when it is insisted that the educator must see the school and society as a whole, to which end the integrated courses in the foundations area are directed. Conant is scathing in his criticism of these "eclectic" courses. Brauner argues that few educationists have sufficient training in the several areas on which such a course must draw, "and shallow are the teams which achieve consensus on such a broad range of ideas." Even those sympathetic with the notion of an integrated foundations course admit the difficulties involved. Harry Broudy, for example, notes the problems raised by the differences in the terminologies, the modes of inquiry, and the nature of evidence in the various disciplines that contribute to such a course:

> It is as if we were trying to locate a city on a dozen maps at once, with each map drawn on different projections and without scales to permit translation from one to the other.[23]

Despite these difficulties, those concepts and findings of the behavioral sciences that have significance for problems of education must be made part of the intellectual equipment of the teacher and administrator in the schools of today. The transmission of these concepts and findings is the responsibility of the professional school, whether the "middleman" be the scholar who is sufficiently knowledgeable about and interested in schools or the educationist who is able and willing to master the methodology and concepts of the

---

21 James Bryant Conant, *The Education of American Teachers* (New York: McGraw-Hill Book Company, 1963), pp. 117–24.

22 Borrowman, *op. cit.,* p. 23.

23 Harry Broudy, "The Use of Cases and Television in Teaching Social Foundations," in *Changes in Teacher Education: An Appraisal,* Report of the Columbus Conference, National Commission on Teacher Education and Professional Standards (Washington, D.C.: National Education Association, 1964), pp. 341–46; see also his "Education of Teachers of Teachers," *Journal of Teacher Education,* XIII (September 1962), 284–91.

fundamental sciences. Furthermore, the results of empirical research alone cannot dictate educational policy; such policy must also be based upon a critical and comprehensive set of values. The dialectic between ideal and fact occupies the center of the problem of educational policy, so much that one of the major responsibilities of foundations programs has been defined as that of providing

> . . . the information, insights, and skills required to: (a) appreciate the powerful educative effect of cultural arrangements; (b) analyze the social realities and democratic ideals of our society; (c) confront these two aspects of American life in a sympathetic, but critical and realistic, appraisal of both our institutional structure and our moral evaluations; and (d) use the results of this appreciation, analysis and confrontation in the formulation and testing of an intelligent conception of the social functions of public education in America.[24]

Brauner's skepticism about "how many professors anywhere in any university could do this for himself [sic], much less teach it to primary and secondary school teachers" appears to ignore the fact that the social functions of the school and changes in society (the drive for equal educational opportunity for racial minorities, for example) do not allow the teacher and the administrator the alternative of avoiding such appraisals. The only questions left open are the quality of the judgments made and the kind of teacher-education program that will be most effective in improving the individual's ability to make such evaluations.

Finally, sound educational policy can seldom be made by taking into account only a single factor; the more significant the policy, the more varied the factors that must be considered. Although the isolation of the historical, sociological, or philosophical aspects of an educational problem produces the advantages of all specialized study, the artificiality of the results gained by such fragmentation is likely to become clear when educational policies are advanced on the assumption that only one type of factor is relevant. The ability to take an integrated point of view cannot be developed by a single course, but it represents an important goal for the teacher-education program and—like all such goals—is most likely to be achieved when deliberately sought and planned for.

---

[24] Archibald Anderson, *et al.*, *The Theoretical Foundations of Education* (Urbana, Ill.: College of Education, Bureau of Educational Research, University of Illinois, 1951), p. 9.

CHAPTER II

Population, Culture, and Values

Universal Education and American Values

The common school. The creation of the common school in America depended, in large part, upon the ability of men who believed in that school to appeal to the requirements of American political and social philosophy.[1] The necessity of universal education in a republic was an argument characterized as trite by Horace Mann when he wrote his annual reports in the 1840's. Because legislators in such a government are, he said, "a mirror reflecting the moral countenance of their constituents, . . . the establishment of a republican government, without well-appointed and efficient means for the universal education of the people, is the most rash and foolhardy experiment ever tried by man."[2] By the 1840's, educators had the persuasive power deriving from the movement to democratize American politics that had developed since Jefferson's unsuccessful Bill for the More General Diffusion of Knowledge (1799). The franchise had been extended: property qualifications for voting had been abolished; the members of the electoral college were no longer chosen by legislators but by the people; presidential candidates were no longer chosen in a congressional caucus but by nominating conventions; and the idea of universal eligibility for public office had won acceptance. These changes provided a substantial justification for an agency that would educate all citizens for the proper exercise of their sovereign power.

The common school won the support of the working classes and their organizations by its promise of equality of opportunity. To Horace Mann, the extent of industrialization and amount of capital in Massachusetts were sufficient cause to fear the "hideous evils" arising from the struggle between capital and labor.

---

[1] Lawrence A. Cremin, *The American Common School* (New York: Teachers College, Bureau of Publications, Columbia University, 1951).

[2] Horace Mann, Twelfth Annual Report (1848), in *The Republic and the School, Horace Mann On the Education of Free Men*, edited by Lawrence A. Cremin (New York: Teachers College, Bureau of Publications, Columbia University, 1957), p. 91.

Now surely, nothing but Universal Education can counterwork this tendency to the domination of capital and the servility of labor. . . . [I]f education be equally diffused, it will draw property after it, by the strongest of all attractions; for such a thing never did happen, and never can happen, as that an intelligent and practical body of men should be permanently poor. Property and labor, in different classes, are essentially antagonistic; but property and labor, in the same class, are essentially fraternal. . . . Education, then, beyond all other devices of human origin, is the great equalizer of the conditions of men—the balance-wheel of the social machinery . . . and, if this education should be universal and complete, it would do more than all things else to obliterate factitious distinctions in society.[3]

Faction also was threatened by the immigrants who began to arrive in great numbers in the decades just before the Civil War, fleeing famine in Ireland and political reaction in Germany. These ethnic enclaves were resented by a society in which strong sentiments of nationalism were beginning to develop. The common school was to function as an instrument of social unification by imbuing native-born American and immigrant with values to which both could give allegiance. Acculturation proved, however, to be not entirely a one-way process; from Germany came Froebel's concept of a kindergarten, which was first incorporated into a public school system in St. Louis in 1873.

The private academy and the public high school. In the second half of the nineteenth century, decisions were made that resulted in the eventual replacement of the private academies by the public high school. As Franklin had envisioned, the breadth and utilitarian purposes of the academy curriculum appealed to a larger group than had the Latin Grammar schools that had constituted secondary education since Colonial days. The academy, however, still secured a large part of its support from tuition; secondary education needed the public support that was being won for the elementary school. But in some states (Michigan, for example) the right of municipalities to tax themselves to support secondary schools remained in question. Justice Cooley's decision in *Stuart* v. *School District No. 1 of the Village of Kalamazoo* (30 Michigan 69, 1874), which found no constitutional objection to such taxation, symbolized the decision to break with the European tradition

---

[3] *Ibid.*, pp. 86, 87.

of a dual educational program and to offer the opportunity for secondary education to all American youth.

The dual system in the United States resulted from the right of private schools to exist alongside the public school system. Paradoxically, affirmation of this right was called forth by the zeal to enforce attendance in public schools. Compulsory attendance laws had been passed in Massachusetts and New York just before the Civil War; thirty more states had such laws by 1900; and by 1918 all the states had them. When the voters of Oregon passed a compulsory education act (1922) making it a misdemeanor for parents of a child eight to sixteen years old to fail to send him to a public school, the U.S. Supreme Court declared the legislation unconstitutional because it conflicted with "the fundamental theory of liberty upon which all governments in this Union repose." This theory, said the Court,

> . . . excludes any general power of the State to standardize its children by forcing them to accept instruction from public teachers only. The child is not the mere creature of the State; those who nurture him and direct his destiny have the right, coupled with the high duty, to recognize and prepare him for additional obligations.[4]

The Kalamazoo decision was based, in part, on the fact that the Michigan constitution had provided for a state university as well as for elementary schools; in the absence of specific prohibition, it seemed appropriate to permit the creation of the intermediate stage of education. A number of state universities had been established before the Civil War, under the stimulus of land grants provided by the Northwest Ordinance of 1787, and of the court decision in *Trustees of Dartmouth College* v. *Woodward* (4 Wheaton 518) in 1819 that meant legislatures must build their own institutions of higher education rather than take over those established under private auspices. State institutions received little support until after the Civil War. The Morrill Act (1862) bestowed on the states some 13 million acres of public land to be used for the creation of mechanical and agricultural colleges which, in twenty-six of the states, were to be combined with the existing state universities. In contrast to the elitist ideal the private liberal arts college had inherited from Colonial days, there developed the idea of a service university

---

[4] *Pierce* v. *Society of Sisters,* 268 U.S. 510 1925.

adapted to the needs of all the citizens of the state. This "democratization" of higher education found expression in a statement by a
Wisconsin State Senate Committee in 1858:

> The farmers, mechanics, miners, merchants, and teachers of Wis-
> consin, represented in this legislature, have a right to ask that this
> bequest of the government shall aid them in securing to themselves
> and their posterity, such educational advantages as shall fit them
> for their pursuits in life, and which by an infusion of intelligence
> and power, shall elevate those pursuits to a social dignity commen-
> surate with their value.[5]

Population Growth, School Attendance, and the Curriculum

Size and rate of population growth.   For such a system of educational opportunity and attendance requirements, three characteristics of the population of the United States 'have been of vital importance: size and rate of growth, age composition, and ethnic
heterogeneity.

Every ten-year period from 1790 to 1960 has seen an increase
in the population of the United States. Except for the war decades
1860–70 and 1910–20, the increase in each period between 1800
and 1930 was greater than that in each previous one. The lowest
rate of population increase occurred in the depression years of the
1930's: the 8.9 million increase reported by the 1940 census represented only a 7.3 per cent gain over 1930. Since that time, however, the trend has been upward. The 1960 population of 180
million reflected a gain of 28 million over that of 1950, an incre-
ment exceeding that of any previous decade in the nation's history,
and the greatest rate of increase (18.5 per cent) since the 1910
census.[6]

For the schools, the age distribution of population is of great importance. Between 1850 and 1950, the proportion of the population
under twenty years old decreased and the proportion of those over
sixty years of age increased. As a consequence, the burden of sup-

---

[5] Quoted by Richard Hofstadter and C. DeWitt Hardy, *The Development and
Scope of Higher Education in the United States* (New York: Columbia University
Press, 1952), p. 46.

[6] U.S. Bureau of the Census, *Our Growing Population*, Graphic Pamphlets, GO
60–1 (Washington, D.C.: USGPO, 1961).

porting the young people in the society was markedly reduced. Since 1940, the population has increased at the extremes of the age span. Between 1950 and 1960, the proportion of those under twenty rose from 34 per cent to 38 per cent of the population; the proportion of those sixty-five and over, from 8.2 per cent to 9.2 per cent. Between 1940 and 1960, the ratio of children and youth to the productive age groups (twenty-two to sixty-four years) rose from 58.6 to 74.2; that of aged citizens to productive age groups, from 11.8 to 16.7. Thus the "dependency ratio," or the average number of dependents each person of productive age is required to support, has steadily increased in the past two decades.[7]

There has also been a steady increase in the proportion of each age group attending school. Of children seven to thirteen years old, less than 50 per cent were attending school in 1850; the proportion rose to 86 per cent in 1910, to 95 per cent in 1930, and to nearly 100 per cent in 1960. The 35 per cent of five- and six-year-olds in school in 1910 rose to 64 per cent in 1960. Startling increases were registered at the secondary school level (public and nonpublic):

School Year	Number Enrolled per 100 Persons 14–17 Years of Age
1889–90	6.7
1899–1900	11.4
1909–10	15.4
1919–20	32.3
1929–30	51.4
1939–40	73.3
1949–50	76.8
1959–60	87.3

Of those eighteen to twenty-one years of age, 4 per cent were in college in 1900, 8 per cent in 1920, 15.6 per cent in 1940, 29.8 per cent in 1950, and 37.2 per cent in 1960.

In the six decades of the twentieth century, the increases in total population and in the proportion attending school have resulted in an increase in school enrollments: from 16.3 million to nearly 33 million in elementary schools, and from approximately 700,000

[7] Eleanor H. Bernert and Charles B. Nam, "Demographic Factors Affecting American Education," in *Social Forces Affecting American Education*, edited by Nelson B. Henry, Sixtieth Yearbook of the National Society for the Study of Education (Chicago: The University of Chicago Press, 1961), pp. 89–119.

to 9.6 million in secondary schools. Degree-credit enrollments in higher education rose during the same period from 238,000 to nearly 3.6 million.

Effect on the curriculum.   The increased range of abilities and interests represented by enrollment increases of this magnitude raised a fundamental problem for the schools, particularly at the secondary school level. The student body changed from a small and highly selected group to almost 90 per cent of the corresponding age group; from students who attended voluntarily to those whose attendance was largely compulsory; and from those preparing for further study in college to those for a majority of whom high school education was terminal. Changes of this kind provided the focal point for a debate that has raged since the last decade of the nineteenth century concerning the kind of curriculum demanded by a democratic social order.

Thus the National Education Association's (NEA) Committee of Fifteen, appointed in 1893 to study the elementary curriculum, recommended an eight-year program cast in terms of subject areas—primarily grammar, arithmetic, geography, and history. Only a few years later John Dewey, in his *School and Society* lectures, pointed out that more than half of the school population left on or before the completion of five years of school, that only 5 per cent entered high school, and that hardly 1 per cent went on to college:

> The simple facts of the case are that in the great majority of human beings the distinctively intellectual interest is not dominant. They have the so-called practical impulse and disposition. . . . Consequently by far the larger number of pupils leave school as soon as they have acquired the rudiments of learning. . . . If we were to conceive our educational end and aim in a less exclusive way, if we were to introduce into educational processes the activities which appeal to those whose dominant impulse is to do and to make, we should find the hold of the school upon its members to be more vital, more prolonged, containing more of culture.[8]

Likewise, it was when those attending high school constituted approximately 10 per cent of the corresponding age group that the curriculum of the high school was "standardized" by the NEA Committee of Ten (1892) and the Committee on College Entrance Re-

---

8 *The School and Society* (1899), *Dewey on Education*, Selections, with an Introduction and Notes, by Martin S. Dworkin (New York: Teachers College, Bureau of Publications, Columbia University, 1959), p. 48.

quirements (1899). The public high school, like the academy, originally conceived its mission to be mainly utilitarian and terminal. As it became almost the only form of secondary education, its college preparatory function grew in importance and the wide variation in the programs offered by the different high schools became a matter of concern to the colleges. As a result of the work of the NEA committees, the proper subjects of the high school curriculum were declared to be language, mathematics, general and natural history, and physics and chemistry. Intensive study of such subjects for four years, said the Committee of Ten, would provide "strong and effective mental training" that would be useful whether the high school student was preparing for the world of work or for college study.

By 1918, however, when approximately 30 per cent of the corresponding age group was attending high school, another NEA committee reviewed the dropout rate in the high schools with deep concern and concluded that curricular changes were necessary. The recommendations of the Committee on the Reorganization of the High School were reminiscent of Herbert Spencer's prescription for an "education for complete living." According to the new report, the curriculum should be organized on the basis of "seven cardinal principles"—health, command of fundamental processes, worthy home membership, vocation, citizenship, worthy use of leisure, and ethical character—ends to which subject matter was to be viewed simply as a means. Thenceforth, the problem was one of developing a curriculum appropriate to what one educator in the 1930's dubbed "the new 50 per cent" of students who could not or would not meet the demands of a college preparatory course, but whose education was the responsibility of the high school. This concern of various investigations, research studies, and educational commissions culminated in the 1940's in the ill-fated program of the Commission on Life Adjustment for Youth.

The trend begun with the "seven cardinal principles" was criticized sharply in the 1930's by William C. Bagley, according to whom American educators, faced with the upward expansion of mass education, had looked about for a philosophy that would "rationalize the loosening of standards and the relaxation of rigor" of the traditional curriculum. This, Bagley thought, accounted for the adoption of theories that he described as emphasizing "interest,

freedom, immediate needs, personal experience, psychological organization, and pupil initiative" and the rejection of theories that
stressed "effort, discipline, remote goals, race experience, logical
sequence, and teacher initiative." Bagley argued that the restoration
of theories of the latter kind as the guiding philosophy of the school
was a necessity if American democracy was to meet the totalitarian
threat from abroad and the challenge of a machine civilization at
home.[9]

The opposing theories described by Bagley referred to a dialectic
familiar to those acquainted with the common themes to be found
in Comenius, Locke, Rousseau, Pestalozzi, and Froebel as they
criticized the schools of their day. With almost monotonous regu-
larity, the educational reformers found schools guilty of verbalism,
neglect of all except purely intellectual education, dependence upon
passive absorption and rote memorization, the organization of materials from the adult's rather than the child's point of view, and the
use of extrinsic rather than intrinsic motivation. Dewey's criticism
of both the traditionalists and the progressives was the negative side
of his effort to hold together the extremes to which Bagley referred.
In his earliest writings on education, Dewey argued that both sides
of the educative process—the psychological and the social—were
indispensable. Although he maintained that the educative process
should take the child's activities as its starting point (lest education
be reduced to "pressure from without"), Dewey defined education
as "a regulation of the process of coming to share in the social consciousness," and in language that should not have offended a Bagley or a Hutchins, would have education make the child "conscious
of its social heritage."[10] The difficulty of successfully maintaining a
position that balanced the two sides of the educational equation,
however, was shown not only by the criticisms that both realists and
idealists continued to level against Dewey but also by the tendency
of progressives themselves to divide into protagonists of either the
child-centered school or social reconstructionism.

---

[9] William C. Bagley, "An Essentialist's Platform for the Advancement of American Education," *Educational Administration and Supervision*, XXIV (April 1938),
244–56.

[10] John Dewey, *My Pedagogic Creed* (1897), Articles I, III, and V.

Ethnic Heterogeneity

The pattern of immigration.   An important aspect of the problem presented by the increased size of the school population was the great variety of cultures it included. Until the 1920's, immigration was a major source of the increases in the population of the United States. Of the 23 million increase in population between 1840 and 1880, 9.5 million were immigrants, as were 5 million of the 13 million increase reported in the 1890 census. The high point of immigration occurred between 1901 and 1910, when 9 million of the 16 million increase for that decade were immigrants. Nearly 6 million more arrived between 1911 and 1920, and another 4 million between 1920 and 1930.

Most of the immigrants who came to the United States prior to the 1880's were from northern and western Europe, although they also included Chinese (brought here during the building of the cross-continental railroads) and Mexicans (who were residents of the territory taken from Mexico after the War of 1846). Between 1910 and 1930, nearly a million more Mexicans were to become migratory agricultural workers or industrial laborers in the North Central States. After 1880, the majority of the immigrants came from southern and eastern Europe, and differed considerably in physical appearance, religion, and cultural background from the native-born and the earlier immigrants. The Japanese did not begin to arrive in significant numbers until after 1898; Filipinos and Puerto Ricans, until after 1920.[11]

The problem of acculturation.   By the end of the first decade of the twentieth century, children of the foreign-born constituted nearly 60 per cent of the school enrollment in the larger cities of the nation; in some cases the proportion was nearly 75 per cent. Cremin suggests that the immigrant character of American society explains, in part, why American schools were more receptive to reform than were European schools. Schools that wanted to educate these children, he says, "could not get by with surface changes." The problem was not merely one of language, but of

> . . . manners, cleanliness, dress, the simple business of getting along together in the schoolroom—these things had to be taught

---

[11] Arnold and Caroline Rose, *America Divided* (New York: Alfred A. Knopf, Inc., 1953), Chap. 2.

more insistently and self-consciously than ever. And long before Spencerian talk about "health," "citizenship," and "ethical character" began to replace "mental discipline" in the ponderous reports of NEA committees, teachers found themselves pursuing these ends in the day-to-day business of teaching.[12]

The schools offered immigrant children the opportunity to learn English and to acquire skills and social attitudes that would enable them to rise from the low social and economic position in which practically all ethnic groups began life in America. The variation in response to this opportunity was, in part, a function of the extent to which the culture of the newcomers differed from that of their adopted land. The value placed upon education in the culture native to the immigrant was an important factor in determining the ease of assimilation. Handlin remarks:

> If the children of Italians in the 1890's and 1920's were inattentive in class, it was not because of want of intelligence, but because of lack of incentive; and that proved more of a problem in their studies than unfamiliarity with English.[13]

The peasant cultures out of which central, southern, and eastern European immigrants came placed a low value upon education. This was also true of the Mexicans, said to be "the least successful in achieving American *arete,* that is, values highly prized in our culture."[14]

The attitude toward education reflects more fundamental value orientations. Florence Kluckhohn has suggested the classification of values on the basis of the solutions chosen by a society to five problems common to all peoples:

> 1. *What is the character of innate human nature?* In various cultures it has been held to be basically evil, of a neutral character, a mixture of good and evil, and essentially good.
> 2. *What is the relation of man to nature (and supernature)?* The major points of view have represented man as subjugated to nature, in harmony with nature, and having mastery over nature.

---

[12] Lawrence A. Cremin, *The Transformation of the School* (New York: Alfred A. Knopf, Inc., 1961), p. 72.

[13] Oscar Handlin, *The Newcomers* (Cambridge, Mass.: Harvard University Press, 1959), p. 27.

[14] Richard E. Gross, *Heritage of American Education* (Boston: Allyn and Bacon, Inc., 1962), p. 370; see also Sister Frances Jerome Woods, *Cultural Values of American Ethnic Groups* (New York: Harper & Row, Publishers, 1956).

3. *What is the temporal focus of human life?* While every society must have a conception of all three dimensions of past, present, and future, societies differ in their "preferential ordering of the alternatives."

4. *What is the modality of human activity?* In the orientation that Kluckhohn calls "Being," the culture prefers "the kind of activity which is a spontaneous expression of what is conceived to be 'given' in the human personality"; the "Being-in-Becoming," like the "Being" orientation, is concerned with "what the human being is rather than what he can accomplish" but stresses the development of "all aspects of the self as an integrated whole"; and the "Doing" orientation demands "the kind of activity which results in accomplishments that are measurable by standards conceived to be external to the acting individual."

5. *What is the modality of man's relationship to other men?* Cultures differ in preferring Lineality (continuity with past generations); Collaterality ("primacy of the goals and welfare of the laterally extended group," e.g., sibling relationships); and Individualism.[15]

The dominant values of American culture, according to Kluckhohn, are those of an evil-but-perfectible definition of human nature; mastery over nature; future; doing; and individualism. Ethnic groups can be represented as variations from the dominant type based on the choice of different solutions to each of the five major problems. The rate and degree of assimilation to American culture of any ethnic group would then depend largely, Kluckhohn points out, upon "the degree of goodness of fit of the group's own rank ordering of value orientations with that of the dominant culture." The contrast between the dominant American value system and the Spanish-American orientation to lineality, the present, subjugation to nature, and being, would help explain the "minimal assimilation" of that ethnic group to American life.

Racial Minorities

Discrimination and the schools. The racial minorities, who have constituted the exception to the assimilationist policies of American society, have provided the deepest challenge to the stated purposes of American education. The attitudes of the dominant

---

[15] Adapted from Florence R. Kluckhohn and Fred L. Strodtbeck, *Variations in Value Orientations* (Evanston, Ill.: Row, Peterson and Company, 1961), pp. 10–19, 24–32.

white group have resulted in discriminatory treatment of nonwhite minorities in housing, employment, political rights, and social relations. In education, the result has been segregated schooling for children of Japanese, Chinese, and Filipino ancestry on the West Coast, and for Mexican-Americans in the West and Southwest. The position of Mexican-Americans and Orientals in American society has resembled that of the largest minority group, the Negro. There operates in the United States what might be described as a caste system: intermarriage between members of different racial groups is outlawed in several states and, on the whole, mobility occurs only within each group. The use of the term *caste* has been opposed on the grounds that, in contrast to India, a set of religious principles justifying such a rigid system of social stratification is lacking in the United States.[16] Whatever the discrepancies between American ideals and actual practice, the basic moral principles of American society deny the concept of caste. Myrdal describes the situation in this country as one in which there are conflicts between moral valuations on various *levels* of consciousness and generality; between the valuations on the "general plane" which he calls "the American Creed,"

> . . . where the American thinks, talks, and acts under the influence of high national and Christian precepts, and, on the other hand, the valuations on specific planes of individual and group living, where personal and local interests, economic, social, and sexual jealousies, considerations of community prestige and conformity, group prejudice against particular persons or types of people, and all sorts of miscellaneous wants, impulses, and habits dominate his outlook.[17]

The schools inevitably have been at the center of this conflict of values. It was ironic that the battle for the common school was "won" in time to face the problem of educating the children of a Negro minority that in 1870 constituted 13.5 per cent of the population of the United States. The roots of that problem lay in the institution of Negro slavery; the economic, political, social, and emotional effects (particularly in the South) of the Civil War and Reconstruction; and the laws passed in the South that prohibited

---

[16] George Eaton Simpson and J. Milton Yinger, *Racial and Cultural Minorities* (New York: Harper & Row, Publishers, 1958), pp. 355–7.

[17] Gunnar Myrdal, *An American Dilemma* (New York: Harper & Row, Publishers, 1944), p. xlvii.

racial intermarriage and legalized segregation. A Louisiana statute requiring segregation on railroad trains was violated by Homer Plessy, "one-eighth Negro," who then instituted an action against the statute on the grounds that such segregation implied the inferiority of the Negro race. The U.S. Supreme Court denied his plea, holding that no damage was experienced as long as the facilities furnished the Negro were equal to those from which he had been excluded (*Plessy* v. *Ferguson,* 163 U.S. 537, 1896). Despite Justice Harlan's dissenting declaration that the Constitution is colorblind, a formula had been found for providing "equality" for the Negro (and for other racial groups), and in the schools as well as in transportation. By 1895, separate schools for Negroes were provided by law in all the former Confederate states, the District of Columbia, Kentucky, Maryland, West Virginia, Delaware, and Missouri; these were joined by Oklahoma in 1907. In the three cases involving education that followed *Plessy* v. *Ferguson,* the last of which (*Gong Lum* v. *Rice,* 277 U.S. 78, 1927) concerned a Chinese girl in Mississippi who—compelled to attend a Negro school—sought admission to a white school, the U.S. Supreme Court avoided direct consideration of the constitutionality of the separate-but-equal doctrine.

Under this doctrine, and despite the efforts of Northern philanthropists after the Civil War, the number of Negro high schools in the South as late as 1916 was relatively small, the students were few, and the curriculum limited and vocationally oriented. State school funds were diverted from Negro to white schools; during the depression of the 1930's, less than 10 per cent of the $200 million granted to the South by the federal government for school construction went for Negro schools. Comparisons of white and Negro schools in the South in 1940 show differentials in favor of the former from the standpoint of current expenditures and capital outlay, teacher-pupil ratios, teacher salaries, and in particular, supplemental services (e.g., library services and transportation).[18] Outside the South—in New Mexico, Arizona, Kansas, and Wyoming—state laws allowed optional segregation; in the North, discrimination in housing laid the foundation for de facto segregation in the schools, a type of segregation also fostered by such practices as gerrymander-

---

[18] Simpson and Yinger, *op. cit.,* pp. 616–19; Richard E. Gross (ed.), *Heritage of American Education* (Boston: Allyn and Bacon, Inc., 1962), pp. 375–81.

ing school district lines and permitting (and encouraging) white pupils to transfer out of predominantly Negro schools.[19] The President's Commission on Higher Education (1947) compared Negroes, foreign-born whites, and native-born whites with respect to amount of schooling completed. At each of the stages in the educational process, from five years of grade school to completion of a four-year college course, the Negro was at the low end of the continuum.[20] At the deeper level of personality, lower-caste status— according to social psychologists—produces a deep feeling of inferiority, a sense of personal humiliation, confusion about personal worth, self-hatred and rejection of one's own group, a defeatist attitude, and a low level of ambition.[21]

The effects of segregation.   These are intangibles, but an interest in the intangible effects of segregation came to characterize the deliberations of the U.S. Supreme Court in a series of cases, beginning in 1938, involving the admission of Negroes to institutions of higher education. Admission to law schools in Missouri and Texas was at issue in two of the cases, and the Court was especially competent to go beyond quantitative considerations and judge the qualitative aspects affecting the "equality" of separate legal education. Thus the Court found substantial inequality between the Negro law school and the University of Texas Law School (which the plaintiff, Herman Sweatt, wished to attend) in size of faculty, number of library volumes, and similar tangible factors. But, in ruling for the plaintiff, the Court declared more important the fact that "the University of Texas Law School possesses to a far greater degree those qualities which are incapable of objective measurement but which make for greatness in a law school" (*Sweatt* v. *Painter*, 339 U.S. 629, 1950). It was not, however, until *Brown* v. *Board of Education* (347 U.S. 483, 1954) that the Court explicitly considered the validity of the separate-but-equal doctrine, and its operation in elementary and secondary education. The decision that "in the field of public education, the doctrine of 'separate but equal' has no place," and that "separate educational facilities are inherently unequal" was anticipated by the U.S. District Court in a Cali-

---

[19] *Public School Segregation and Integration in the North* (Washington, D.C.: National Association of Intergroup Relations Officials, 1963), p. 7.

[20] President's Commission on Higher Education, *Higher Education for American Democracy* (Washington, D.C.: USGPO, 1947), Vol. II, p. 30.

[21] *Public School Segregation and Integration in the North, op. cit.,* p. 33.

fornia case (*Mendez* v. *Westminster School District,* 1946). In outlawing the segregation of Mexican-Americans in public schools, the U.S. District Court declared social equality to be "a paramount requisite in the American system of public education." That system, the decision said, "must be open to all children by unified school association regardless of lineage."

In *Brown* v. *Board of Education,* the Supreme Court noted that its decision could not be made on the basis of tangible factors, for the Negro and white schools involved in the case had been or were being equalized in these respects.

> We must look instead to the effect of segregation itself on public education. . . . Today, education is perhaps the most important function of state and local governments. Compulsory school attendance laws and the great expenditures for education both demonstrate our recognition of the importance of education to our democratic society. It is required in the performance of our most basic public responsibilities, even service in the armed forces. It is the very foundation of good citizenship. Today it is a principal instrument in awakening the child to cultural values, in preparing him for later professional training, and in helping him to adjust normally to his environment. In these days, it is doubtful that any child may reasonably be expected to succeed in life if he is denied the opportunity of an education. Such an opportunity, where the state has undertaken to provide it, is a right which must be made available to all on equal terms.

Whatever may have been the extent of psychological knowledge at the time of *Plessy* v. *Ferguson,* the Court declared, it is now known that to separate children in grade school and high school "from others of similar age and qualifications solely because of their race generates a feeling of inferiority as to their status in the community that may affect their hearts and minds in a way unlikely ever to be undone."

After hearing suggestions from the parties on the nature of the remedy that should be prescribed, the Court, on May 31, 1955, remanded the cases to the courts that originally heard them, with the request that they "take such proceedings and enter such orders and decrees consistent with this opinion as are necessary and proper to admit to public schools on a racially nondiscriminatory basis with all deliberate speed the parties to these cases."

Integration trends.   As these instructions have been carried out, they have raised the broader issue of the extent to which the schools could provide leadership in reforming the culture pattern of racial discrimination involving both whites and nonwhites. In the South, the schools have been largely unsuccessful, over the ten-year period since the decision, in operating in contravention of the mores of that region. In 1964, only 1.06 per cent of the Negro children in the eleven Southern states were in school with whites, although this ranged from a policy of complete noncompliance in Mississippi to desegregated schooling for 4.29 per cent of the Negro children in Texas. In the six border states and the District of Columbia, however, 56.2 per cent of the Negro children were in school with whites; and all the institutions of higher education in the border states, and 115 of the 212 in the Southern states, were desegregated, at least on a token basis.

Statistics on the mixture of "compliance, tokenism, and defiance"[22] in the border and Southern areas hardly indicate the deep social convulsions and the personal ordeal of children and educators produced by this attempt at the "reconstruction of society" through the schools. In preparing for disbursement of federal education grants for 1965–66, the U.S. Office of Education is able to employ the provisions of Title VI of the Civil Rights Act of 1964 to bring pressure for desegregated schooling on school boards which must provide assurances of compliance if they are to participate in such grants. But assurances of compliance are not identical with compliance, just as desegregation is not the same as integration. For both North and South, it has become increasingly clear that the success of the educational effort depends upon fundamental changes in the values and institutions of the society as a whole.

---

[22] Jim Leeson, "The First Ten Years," *Phi Delta Kappan* XLV (May 1964), 362–70.

CHAPTER III

Social Stratification

Social Class in America

The "classless" society. The common school promised the individual equality of opportunity—a means of determining his status, not through inherited wealth and position, but by energy and ability. During a large part of the nineteenth century, the frontier and an expanding economy played an important part in assuring social mobility. In combination with an individualistic ideology, these characteristics of the American environment produced the image of a "classless" society in the minds of Americans and foreigners as well. Except for sociologists, early American social scientists (unlike European scholars) exhibited little interest in social class, and even the sociologists were highly influenced by the "anticlass elements of American democracy, and by the social virtues of that 'classless' segment of society—the middle class."[1] In the 1930's, however, Page was able to note a greater interest in problems of social stratification and mobility, and a transition from theorizing to empirical investigation in the work of Sorokin, the Lynds, and Dollard.

It was during that decade that an influential body of work by W. Lloyd Warner and his associates produced a methodology for the analysis of social-class differences and a description of the social-class structure of American communities in New England (Yankee City), the South (Old City), and the Midwest (Jonesville). These investigators asserted that in American society, as in all societies of any complexity, differentiation of functions results in the development of different statuses, and that these divisions (and the individuals belonging to them) may be discovered by interviewing people in the community—"the final authorities about the realities of American social class."[2] *Social classes* were defined by Warner as

[1] Charles H. Page, *Class and American Sociology: From Ward to Ross* (New York: The Dial Press, Inc., 1940), pp. 249–52.

[2] W. Lloyd Warner, Marchia Meeker, and Kenneth Eells, *Social Class in America* (New York: Harper & Row, Publishers, 1960), p. 38. Reprinted by permission of W. Lloyd Warner.

"two or more orders of people who are believed to be, and are accordingly ranked by the members of the community, in socially superior and inferior positions."[3] Warner rejected the attempt to define *social class* solely in "objective" terms, although he devised a rating system (Index of Status Characteristics) that used occupation, source of income, type of house, and neighborhood as indices of social position. But, he warned:

> . . . social and economic factors, such as talent, income, and money, if their potentialities for rank are to be realized, must be translated into social-class behavior acceptable to the members of any given social level of the community.[4]

A social class, that is, represents a way of life, a subculture, with special values, interests, traditions, and participation patterns, of which the "blueblood" for example, cannot be divested by a sudden decrease in income, any more than the *nouveau riche* can automatically acquire them.

Social-class patterns. The most stable and elaborate class system was found in the East and the South; both in Yankee City and in Old City not only were the middle- and lower-class groups divided into two subgroups of upper and lower, but a similar division held for the upper class, based on lineage or the possession of "old" as distinguished from "new" wealth. The Midwestern community (Jonesville), on the other hand, did not have an upper-upper class. A generalized picture of the class structure, from upper to lower, as portrayed by the Warner studies, shows:

    1. A shift from "pure stock" to classes in which ethnic groups and color castes are in the majority;
    2. A steady decrease in amount of wealth, value of property owned, and size and condition of homes;
    3. A decrease in the proportion of older people and in marriage age; an increase in number of children;
    4. A tendency for professional, financial, and proprietary personnel to predominate in the upper classes; owners of small business, managers, clerks, and skilled workers, in the middle classes; and semiskilled and unskilled workers, in the lower classes;
    5. Variation in prestige according to area of residence; indeed, the community often refers to classes by the name of street or area: the "Hillstreeters" (upper-class), the "Sidestreeters" (lower-mid-

---

[3] W. Lloyd Warner and Paul S. Lunt, *The Social Life of a Modern Community* (New Haven: Yale University Press, 1941), p. 82.
[4] Warner, Meeker, and Eells, *op. cit.,* p. 39.

dle class), and the "Riverbrookers" or "Boxtowners" (lower-lower-class);

6. A tendency for religious affiliations to go from Protestant to Catholic, with regional differences determining variations in the class ranking of Protestant sects;

7. An increase of arrests and police reports—more, admittedly, a measure of the ability of parents to protect the members of their families from outside interference than of differences in criminal tendencies among classes.[5]

The work of Warner and his associates has been criticized both in conception and in methodology, and the potential for generalization of findings in a few communities to American society as a whole has been questioned. The more rural the area, the less do Warner's class categories seem to fit. As early as 1944, however, Allison Davis denied that there is a uniform number of social classes in American communities. The size, age, rate of growth, economic complexity, and ethnic composition of the community were admitted to affect the character of social stratification.[6] Nevertheless, there are striking similarities between the class structure portrayed by the Warner group and that based on a still continuing study by Hodges in the area from San Francisco to San Jose.[7] The proportion of the population within each class in a given community is affected by the nature of the community: a heavily industrialized city, for instance, presents a different picture from a wealthy residential suburb. In general, however, about 2 per cent of Americans are upper-class; 8 per cent, upper-middle-class; 30 per cent, lower-middle-class; 40 per cent, upper-lower-class; and 20 per cent, lower-lower-class.[8] Bergel, after reviewing criticisms and alternatives to the Warner approach, concluded that Warner has come closest to solving the problem of finding a scale that is "neither too elementary nor too complex," one that not only provides "an excellent

---

[5] Adapted from W. Lloyd Warner, *American Life, Dream and Reality* (Chicago: The University of Chicago Press, 1962), pp. 74–79. Warner and Lunt, *op. cit.,* Chaps. 20–22.

[6] W. Lloyd Warner, Robert J. Havighurst, and Martin Loeb, *Who Shall Be Educated?* (New York: Harper & Row, Publishers, 1944), pp. 29–32.

[7] Harold Hodges, "Peninsula People: Social Stratification in a Metropolitan Complex," in *Education and Society,* edited by W. Warren Kallenbach and Harold M. Hodges, Jr. (New York: Charles E. Merrill Books, Inc., 1963), pp. 389–422.

[8] Robert J. Havighurst, "Social Class Influences on American Education," in *Social Forces Affecting American Education,* edited by Nelson B. Henry, Sixtieth Yearbook of the National Society for the Study of Education (Chicago: The University of Chicago Press, 1961), p. 121.

working proposition ('statistical' classes) but fairly depicts the actual situation ('social' classes)," providing one assumes that sharp divisions between the six classes do not exist.[9]

Social Class and Success in School

The dropout problem.   Early studies of the effect of social class upon education carefully documented the contrast between the school record of youths of lower social status and those of higher social status: the early beginning and high rate of school dropouts among lower-class youths, their concentration in nonacademic curricula, their higher failure rate, and their lower participation in extracurricular activities.[10] More recent data are provided by Sexton's study of Big City, a Midwestern community described as one of the largest and, by many standards, the most prosperous in the country;[11] and Havighurst's longitudinal study of youth from the sixth grade through the first college year, in River City, a Midwestern community of nearly 45,000 residents.[12]

In the Big City elementary schools, the dropout rate for children in the lowest-income group was twenty-two times as great as that of children in the highest income group. In the senior high school, in a one-year period, dropouts in the schools where the average family income was below $7000 represented 17.8 per cent of total registration; in schools where the average family income exceeded $7000, the dropout rate was only 6.3 per cent. In River City, 46 per cent of the dropouts came from the lower-lower class, compared with 13 per cent of those who stayed in school. Of the upper-class students, only one in twenty dropped out of high school, and four out of five went on to college. Only two of the fifty-seven boys, and none of the girls, in the lowest social class went to college.

Promotion and failure. Not unexpectedly, differences in achievement continued to parallel differences in amount of schooling. As measured by the tests given to Big City children, not only

[9] Egon Ernest Bergel, *Social Stratification* (New York: McGraw-Hill Book Company, 1962), p. 259.

[10] August Hollingshead, *Elmtown's Youth* (New York: John Wiley & Sons, Inc., 1949), pp. 172, 173, 201, 330, 332, 462; Warner and Lunt, *op. cit.,* p. 364.

[11] Patricia Sexton, *Education and Income* (New York: The Viking Press, Inc., 1961).

[12] Robert J. Havighurst, *et al., Growing Up in River City* (New York: John Wiley & Sons, Inc., 1962).

did achievement scores in the elementary schools rise with family income levels, they also showed a cumulative effect, the differences between the lowest- and highest-income groups becoming greater with each school grade. Most recently, a study of the Harlem schools showed a similar pattern: third-grade pupils in central Harlem were fully one year behind the achievement levels of other New York City third-grade pupils; by the sixth grade, they were nearly two years behind; by the eighth grade, two and one half years. The longer these pupils are in school, then, the greater the proportion that fail to meet comparative norms of achievement.[13]

In the Big City elementary schools in January 1958, the number of students in the lowest-income group schools who failed to be promoted was ten times that in the highest-income group schools. A comparison of a less privileged school in River City with a school from a predominantly upper-middle-class district with respect to failure rate, quality of grades in academic subjects, and school averages at the time of high school graduation, likewise showed the students from the less privileged school significantly lower in achievement. In Big City, as in Yankee City and Elmtown, the lower-middle- and lower-class groups were predominantly in the nonacademic curricula. The effect of the guidance function of the junior high school, where electives and departmentalization are first encountered, is, according to Martin Mayer,

> . . . to solidify the structure of class bias—those who elect an academic program will be business executive and professional people, while those who elect the "general" or "business" program will be clerks, and those who elect a "vocational" program will work with their hands.[14]

That "pupils of the lower classes will experience frustration and failure and pupils of the higher classes will experience gratification and success in their educational experience," says W. W. Charters Jr. in a recent summary of research, is a conclusion supported by overwhelming evidence.[15] He adds immediately, however, that this

---

[13] Unpublished report, summarized in the Special Education Survey, *The New York Times* (January 16, 1964), 87.

[14] Martin Mayer, *The Schools* (New York: Harper & Row, Publishers, 1961), p. 323.

[15] W. W. Charters, Jr., "The Social Background of Teaching," in *Handbook of Research and Teaching,* edited by N. L. Gage (Chicago: Rand McNally & Co., 1963), p. 739.

holds true for groups, not necessarily for individuals. From the earliest to the latest research, the data have indicated exceptions to the
influence of social class. Nevertheless, there continues to be a high
correlation between social class and success in school. To an un-
determined extent, this is the result of the position of the Negro in
the American society. A comparison of the incidence of Negro and
white dropouts in Detroit secondary schools in 1960–61 showed
the median percentage of withdrawals from predominantly Negro
junior high schools to be about 43 per cent larger than that in the
predominantly white junior high schools; and in the senior high
school, where the restrictions of compulsory attendance laws are
not as severe, the median percentage for the Negro schools was two
and a half times as large as that for predominantly white schools.[16]

Social Class and Ability

Culturally biased tests.   According to Hollingshead, the lack of
school success on the part of Elmtown's lower-class youths was not
the result of lack of intelligence. Although he admitted a "significant
association" of intelligence with class position, he denied that the
degree of association was high enough to account for the concentration of course failures among the students of lowest status, or
for the high grades awarded high-status students.[17] Based on the data
gathered on Pennsylvania school children in the 1920's, Sibley concluded that at the ninth- and twelfth-grade level, intelligence had
more influence than father's status on educational opportunity, but
that the situation was sharply reversed at the college level, where
intelligent boys had only a four-to-one advantage over the least
intelligent, but sons of men in the highest occupational level enjoyed
an advantage of more than ten to one over those from the lowest
level. Sibley's data, however, showed that even on the lower levels
of education, a perfect fit of educational opportunity and ability
(as measured by IQ score) was not achieved; for example, of the
boys with an IQ under 88, 64 per cent from the highest occupational group completed twelve or more grades, compared with 25

[16] *Public School Segregation and Integration in the North* (Washington, D.C.:
National Association of Intergroup Relations Officials, 1963), pp. 37–39.
[17] Hollingshead, *op. cit.,* pp. 172–75.

per cent from the lowest occupational group.[18] The more recent studies by Sexton and Havighurst have shown similar results. Havighurst, for example, found a close connection between intellectual ability and school progress, but "an even closer connection between social class and school progress."[19]

According to investigators at the University of Chicago, these conclusions still underplay the effects of social class because they are based upon the results of culturally biased intelligence tests. That intelligence tests reflect class bias was shown by Allison Davis, who was able to raise the percentage of correct responses made by lower socioeconomic groups by changing the vocabulary in test questions from one that favored middle-class experience to one that involved simpler terms.[20] Even the picture tests used by Big City schools, Sexton remarks,[21] were class-biased in that they demanded recognition of animals (particularly zoo animals) and objects (violins, ocean liners) not within the experience of the lower-class child. Studies of lower-class children have revealed a much more restricted "life space" than that of middle-class children who have the advantage of vacation travel and visits to symphony concerts, art museums, and the like. Some of the children attending Paul Lawrence Dunbar School, an elementary school in a Negro slum in Philadelphia, come to kindergarten without knowing their own names, and many have vocabularies so limited they cannot speak in sentences.

> . . . [Their experiences are] so limited that stories in their primers will not make sense to them. The majority of these children—and many of the parents—have not been farther from their tenement homes than twenty-five blocks. They have not seen motion pictures, eaten in a restaurant, or ridden in a bus; they have never lived in a situation where a mother and father work together to rear a family. Of course they do not identify with the middle-class Dicks and Janes in the typical reading books.[22]

---

[18] Elbridge Sibley, "Some Demographic Clues to Stratification," *American Sociological Review*, VII (June 1942), 322–30.

[19] Havighurst, *et al., op. cit.,* pp. 22–23, 52.

[20] Allison Davis, *Social Class Influence Upon Learning* (Cambridge, Mass.: Harvard University Press, 1948).

[21] Sexton, *op. cit.,* pp. 43–47.

[22] Aleda Druding, "Stirrings in the Big Cities: Philadelphia," *National Education Association Journal*, LI, 2 (February 1962), 48. Reprnted by permission of the author.

  "Culture-free" tests. Riessman claims that there is a "hidden IQ and a hidden personality" that the test and even the clinical interview does not reveal.[23] He stresses the effect of a simple lack of "school know-how" on the success of lower-class children on IQ tests, and points out that the testing situation is a social situation, in which "the attitude of the children toward the test situation and the examiner" may be even more important than the content of the test items. Children from different cultural backgrounds respond differently to the idea of being tested. As Hollingshead points out, the culture of children from the middle and upper classes imbues them with a need for personal achievement that causes them to respond positively and aggressively to competitive situations, whereas lower-class children come from a background in which "failure, worry, and frustrations are common," and in which the relationship between school grades and success in life has not been emphasized. In their stress on verbal relationships, complex academic phrasing, rare vocabularies, and stress on speed of reaction, IQ tests work particularly against the "cognitive style" of the deprived child, a style which, according to Riessman, is typically

1. Physical and visual rather than aural;
2. Content-centered rather than form-centered;
3. Externally oriented rather than introspective;
4. Problem-centered rather than abstract-centered;
5. Inductive rather than deductive;
6. Spatial rather than temporal;
7. Slow, careful, patient, persevering (in areas of importance) rather than quick, clever, facile, flexible.[24]

  The attempt of Davis and Eells to develop a "culture-free" intelligence test appears, however, to have failed, and the logic of developing a test that would minimize differential achievement of desirable objectives (verbal and linguistic skills, for example) has been questioned. In Charters' opinion, the chief value of the criticism of IQ tests from the anthropological point of view has been to warn educators against interpreting IQ scores as reflecting innate limitations on the child's mental abilities; such criticism has "helped

---

[23] Frank Riessman, *The Culturally Deprived Child* (New York: Harper & Row, Publishers, 1962), p. 51.

[24] *Ibid.,* p. 73; see also p. 67 and Chap. 8.

to remove the bias, if not from the tests, at least from the test users in the educational profession."[25]

Social Class and the Conflict of Values

Social-class values.   In explaining the effects of social class upon school success, early investigators appeared to describe the treatment given the lower-class student by teachers and administrators as the result of a deliberate policy based on class snobbery. One of the reasons given by Elmtown youths who dropped out of school was "mistreatment by teachers"—a mistreatment Hollingshead described as taking various forms, ranging from outright favoritism toward upper-class children in the awarding of grades and prizes to the harsher enforcement of disciplinary rules upon lower-class children. In some elementary schools in Old City, students were rated and placed in an A, B, or C section, ostensibly on the basis of ability; teachers were quite aware, however, that the sections reflected social-class distinctions.[26]

Warner attributes most of such treatment to "ignorance of social class and how it operates in our lives"; it is unintentional unfairness arising from the fact that the teacher is a product of the same class system. Teachers are predominantly middle-class, and hence apply middle-class values in rating children. For the teacher "upper- and upper-middle-class children possess traits that rank high and are positive; lower-class children have characteristics that are negative and are ranked low."[27]

In Kluckhohn's terminology, the lower class is oriented toward the present, being and either individualism or collaterality, in contrast to the middle-class orientation toward the future, doing, and individualism.[28] Allison Davis has compared middle- and lower-class people with respect to the three basic values of property, sex, and aggression.[29] He contrasts the high value placed upon the acquisition

[25] W. W. Charters, Jr. "Social Class and Intelligence Tests," in *Readings in the Social Psychology of Education,* edited by W. W. Charters, Jr., and N. L. Gage (Boston: Allyn and Bacon, Inc., 1963), p. 21.

[26] Warner, Havighurst, and Loeb, *op. cit.,* pp. 73–74.

[27] Warner, Meeker, and Eells, *op. cit.,* p. 28.

[28] Florence R. Kluckhohn and Fred L. Strodtbeck, *Variations in Value Orientations* (Evanston, Ill.: Row, Peterson and Company, 1961), p. 27.

[29] Allison Davis, "American Status Systems and the Socialization of the Child," *American Sociological Review,* VII (1941), 345–54.

and accumulation of property and upon the related virtues of thrift and hard work by the Puritan ethic of the middle-class person with the light-hearted attitude toward property rights which the lower-class child learns from his family and street culture. Respectability, conformity to community standards, and emotional control typify the middle classes, whereas the lower classes do not regard sexual drives and behavior as inherently taboo and dangerous, and the family of the lower-class girl often fails to provide a very good example of sexual inhibition. Finally, the middle class teaches adolescents to disguise their aggressions as initiative or ambition in order to compete effectively by means of social and economic skills, whereas the lower-class adolescent is rewarded—by his family, play group, or gang—for superiority in techniques of physical aggression.

Teacher-student relationships. The effect of such conflicting values upon teacher-student relationships was revealed by Becker's study of Chicago school teachers.[30] For those in service occupations, according to Becker, the nature of the work and techniques of performance are conceived in terms of the image of an "ideal" client, and problems arise for such personnel when actual clients deviate from this image. The cultural diversity resulting from social-class differences constitutes one source of the discrepancy between ideal and actual "client" for the teacher. The Chicago teachers Becker interviewed mentioned three problems in particular: teaching itself, discipline, and moral acceptability. In each case the lower-class "client" presented serious problems: disinterest in learning, misbehavior, and offensiveness because of dishonesty, bad health habits, loose sexual attitudes, and obscenity. Teachers have been found to be less favorably inclined toward even those deprived children whose school achievement is good, and thereby have affected adversely the achievement and classroom behavior of the lower-class child.[31] According to a case study reported by a Stanford research team, a fifth-grade teacher of middle-class origin contradicted in his performance his own professed aims and even his own beliefs about what he actually did in the classroom. Observation of this teacher revealed a consistent, although unconscious, bias against

---

[30] Howard S. Becker, "Social Class Variations in the Teacher-Pupil Relationship," *Journal of Educational Sociology,* XXV (April 1952), 451–65.

[31] Reissman, *op. cit.,* p. 18.

students of lower socioeconomic class that seriously interfered with his ability to communicate effectively with them.[32]

Wattenberg, however, warns against an oversimplified interpretation of the effect of social-class background on teacher behavior, pointing out that such background will have a different meaning for people of different personality structures. Teachers who come from poor families, for example, may exhibit different patterns: one may regard his origin as something to be "lived down," another may ally himself with pupils and parents of similar origin, a third may be unusually strict and even punitive against children of the same socioeconomic status. Likewise, a middle-class teacher from an easy-going home may find little difficulty in getting along well with lower-status children, whereas one with a more rigid upbringing may exhibit various religious, ethnic, or racial prejudices. Wattenberg regards the increased social range from which he believes teachers—especially urban teachers at the secondary school level—are being recruited to be a hopeful sign for the possibilities of finding teachers who are able to work well with lower-class pupils. There still is, he believes, a shortage of those who can deal on the basis of full understanding with such children, particularly in the elementary school where the child's reactions to school are formed.[33]

Social Class and Aspirational Level

Social mobility. The upward mobility of lower-class children is impaired to a certain degree, Bergel asserts, by the low value the lower classes place upon education. Or, as Hyman puts it, "the lower-class individual doesn't want as much success, knows he couldn't get it even if he wanted to, and doesn't want what might help him get success."[34] Apart from external factors beyond the control of even a highly motivated individual, "this value system

---

[32] George D. Spindler, "The Transmission of American Culture," in *Education and Culture,* edited by George D. Spindler (New York: Holt, Rinehart & Winston, Inc., 1963), pp. 148–72.

[33] William Wattenberg, "Social Origin and Teaching Role: Some Typical Patterns," in *The Teacher's Role in American Society,* edited by Lindley J. Stiles, Sixteenth Yearbook of the John Dewey Society (New York: Harper & Row, Publishers, 1957), p. 31.

[34] Herbert H. Hyman, "The Value Systems of Different Classes: A Sociopsychological Contribution to the Analysis of Stratification," in *Class, Status, and Power,* edited by Richard Bendix and Seymour Lipset. Copyright 1953 by The Free Press of Glencoe, a Corporation. Reprinted by permission.

would create a self-imposed barrier to an improved position." Thus, a 1947 National Opinion Research Center poll of 2500 adults regarding their attitudes toward education revealed that 39 per cent of those rated by the interviewer as lower-class recommended a college education, compared with 52 per cent of the middle-class group and 68 per cent of the wealthy and prosperous.

Neither parent nor peer group in the lower class ordinarily emphasizes the value of education to the child; and a majority of the students who drop out of high school have parents who have not completed high school. Parental influence has been investigated by Kahl, who analyzed the data obtained by a questionnaire administered to boys in public high schools in eight towns in the Boston metropolitan area, to show the independent operation of social class (as measured by father's occupation), intelligence, and aspiration.[35] The results showed that 56 per cent of those in the lowest IQ quintile but in the highest occupational status expected to go to college, as compared with 29 per cent of those in the highest IQ quintile but of the lowest occupational status. The investigators were particularly interested in the boys in the lower-middle levels—the "common-man" group, in Warner's terminology—a combination of lower-middle and upper-lower classes. Although these boys had enough intelligence to aim high, they were not from families that took college attendance for granted, and so were forced to make a conscious decision at some stage in their careers. Interviews with twenty-four boys (and their families), twelve of whom were in college preparatory courses and definitely planned to go to a regular academic college after high school, and twelve of whom did not, revealed the division to stem from differences in parental attitudes. Kahl concluded that, within the "common-man" class, some accept the American creed—"belief in getting ahead"—and some believe in just "getting by." The latter fit the description Bergel gives of the "ambition" of the lowest classes:

> . . . [It is] largely negative: not to be bothered, not to be irritated, not to worry about consequences. It is not so much apathy . . . as acceptance of given conditions and lack of ambition. That goes for their children, too. They want their children to earn a living as soon as possible and prefer jobs that will not be too exacting.

[35] J. A. Kahl, "Educational and Occupational Aspirations of 'Common Man' Boys," *Harvard Educational Review*, XXIII (Summer 1953), 186–203.

> Therefore children are not encouraged to spend more time in school than necessary; improvements, mostly in terms of wages, are desirable but not at the expense of mental exertion. . . . They derive partial compensation for what they lose by being spared the anguish of competition, the frustrations of failure, and the nervous tension invariably resulting from responsibility.[36]

This is what Kluckhohn means when she says that low-status people tend to be oriented to the present rather than to the future; or in Schneider and Lysgaard's phraseology, they lack the "deferred gratification pattern" demanded by the longer period of preparation for high-status positions.[37] Coleman suggests that social class affects educational achievement by the development of such a pattern rather than directly through the social snobbishness of children and teachers.[38]

Educational achievement. The tendency from earlier to later investigators has been to shift the responsibility for the unsuccessful school experience of the lower-class child from the school itself to the culture of the low-status family. Havighurst has recently referred apologetically to *Elmtown's Youth* as a product of the "muckraking" period of social class analysis.[39] Questions have been raised, however, about the gain to the school of shifting from the fatalism of the IQ score to the fatalism of the Index of Status Characteristics. Riessman criticizes the Higher Horizons program sharply for claiming that the school is the only positive experience in the life of the culturally deprived child. Properly understood, he asserts, the cultural approach includes a "genuine respect for the efforts of the deprived in coping with difficult life conditions"; and the school, if only on pragmatic grounds, must not look solely at the failures and weaknesses, but seek to build upon the strengths possessed by the lower-class culture: "the extended family, the cooperative and equalitarian tradition, the anger and alienation, the desire for structure, the informality and humor."[40]

Livingstone reminds us that there are "contemporary" as well as "historical" components in the decision by a particular student to

---

[36] Bergel, *op. cit.,* pp. 406–407.
[37] Louis Schneider and Sverre Lysgaard, "The Deferred Gratification Pattern: A Preliminary Study," *American Sociological Review,* XVIII (April 1953), 142–49.
[38] James S. Coleman, *The Adolescent Society* (New York: The Free Press of Glencoe, Inc., 1961), p. 105, fn. 4.
[39] Havighurst, *op. cit.,* p. viii.
[40] Riessman, *op. cit.,* pp. 105–106, 128–29.

drop out of school. The basic factor, he suggests, may be the value the youth has come to place on education and "the perceived relevance" of education to his goals. "This value is the contemporary result of the interplay of forces in his environment as he has matured."[41] There are educators who prefer to speak of *pushouts* rather than *dropouts,* and who refuse to believe that a high retention rate is good in itself. Although it provides experiences that offset the influence of the nonschool environment on the potential dropout, the school may also contribute to the dropout problem. The 70 per cent of the dropouts who have at least average intelligence and could complete high school, and the 6–13 per cent who could do college work, have been characterized as "victims of economic, social, cultural, and psychological pressures which they have not been able to cope with alone. They are rejecting a situation that they feel has rejected them."[42] It would be regrettable if the cultural approach were employed to relieve the school of its responsibilities, rather than to provide the means by which those responsibilities may be more completely fulfilled.

---

[41] A. Hugh Livingstone, "The Dropout: A Challenge to the Schools," *Administrator's Notebook,* VI, 5 (January 1958).

[42] Eli E. Cohen, Executive Secretary of the National Committee on the Employment of Youth, "Urban Youth Employment Needs Today," 1962 (mimeographed).

CHAPTER IV

Economics, Technology, and Education

Economic Productivity and Mass Education

The rise in productivity. One of the most important factors making possible the experiment in mass education in the United States has been the level of productivity of the economy. Recent U.S. Bureau of Labor Statistics show the average annual increase in output per manhour over the last half-century has been 2.4 per cent; since 1947, 3 per cent; and in the period 1960–63, 3.6 per cent. Agriculture has been called "the pace-setter in the productivity contest." Farm output, measured against manhours, increased 80 per cent during the decade 1948–58, or at a cumulative rate of 6 per cent as compared with a 2.5 per cent increase for the nonfarm sector.[1] Between 1950 and 1961, the amount of sown acreage decreased about 12 per cent and the number of farm workers 30 per cent; because farm output increased 24 per cent in the same period, each farm worker was supplying almost twice as many people as in 1950.[2] In manufacturing, productivity per manhour increased about 3 per cent each year between 1909 and 1939. Between 1900 and 1950, while average weekly work hours decreased from 60.2 to 40, net output per manhour increased from $0.602 to $1.935, and total national income (at 1950 prices) rose from $60 billion to $217 billion.[3] More than four fifths of the 50 per cent increase in the real output of the entire private economy since World War II has been attributed to an increase in output per manhour.

Such a productivity record has increased resources for the support of education, and has enabled individuals to postpone entry into the production of goods and services. These effects are reflected not only in the increased proportion of school-age groups

---

[1] Harold Groves, *Education and Economic Growth* (Washington, D.C.: National Education Association, 1961), p. 19.

[2] *Road Maps of Industry*, No. 1408 (New York: National Industrial Conference Board, December 21, 1962).

[3] Newton Edwards and Herman G. Richey, *The School in the American Social Order* (Boston: Houghton Mifflin Company, 1963), p. 416.

actually in school but also in increased educational attainment in the population. Approximately 70 per cent of the secondary school age group graduated in 1963, as compared with about 9 per cent in 1910. Sixty-four per cent of the population in the twenty-five-to-thirty-four group are high school graduates, compared with 32 per cent of those in the fifty-five-to-sixty-four group.[4]

The advance of technology. Past and projected productivity increases are based upon the development and application of an increasingly sophisticated technology both in agriculture and in industry. Groves describes the agricultural achievement as a "chemical revolution on top of a biological revolution on top of an engineering revolution."[5] The increased productivity in the economy at large is related to the development of cybernation—or the use, in combination, of automation and computers. Does the "cybercultural revolution" represent merely the "latest stage in the evolution of technological means for removing the burden of work," or is it "so different in degree as to be a profound difference in kind"?[6] Does it mean a radical reduction in employment opportunities, or does it only make it possible "to do many things which otherwise could not and would not be done"?[7] These are still debatable issues that should be of profound interest to educators concerned about the shape of the society and the school program of the future.

The schools are not merely acted upon by economic, scientific, and technological forces; they have helped to create and to shape these forces. Groves calls attention to the significance, for the fabulous achievements of American agriculture, of the funds expended on research and on the dissemination of research findings through the land-grant colleges. He quotes Sumner Schlichter's observation that one of the most revolutionary economic developments of the last century has been the discovery that an enormous amount of research can be carried on for profit. Groves' study for the National Education Association is just one example of an increasing interest on the part of economists in the relationship between education and eco-

---

[4] *Road Maps of Industry,* No. 1418 (New York: National Industrial Conference Board, March 1, 1963).

[5] Groves, *op. cit.,* p. 20.

[6] Donald M. Michael, *Cybernation: The Silent Conquest* (Santa Barbara, Calif.: Center for the Study of Democratic Institutions, Ford Foundation for the Republic, 1962), p. 5.

[7] Yale Brozen, "Automation: The Impact of Technological Change," *Chicago,* I, 1 (Fall 1963), p. 16.

nomic growth, an interest that has been stimulated by the problem of the developing nations.[8]

Occupational Trends, Youth, and Unemployment

The transformation of the labor force. One result of the increased productivity of the American economy is the transformation of the labor force, shown in the following comparisons (made by Seymour L. Wolfbein, Deputy Assistant Secretary of Labor) of trends in occupational distribution between 1910 and 1959:[9]

	1910	1959	1970
White-collar workers	22	42	45
Professional and technical	5	11	13
Proprietary and managerial	7	11	11
Clerical and sales	10	20	21
Blue-collar workers	37	37	36
Skilled	12	13	13
Semiskilled	14	18	18
Unskilled	11	6	5
Service workers	10	12	13

It will be noted that all subdivisions of white-collar workers increased as a proportion of the total labor force in the period 1910–59. Although the proportion of blue-collar workers underwent little change, there was a marked decline in the proportion of unskilled workers. It is noteworthy also that there are now more persons in service industries (32.5 million) than in goods-producing industries (26 million). Most significant has been the decline of agricultural workers from 50 per cent of the labor force in 1870 to 31 per cent in 1910 to 9 per cent in 1959 to an estimated 6 per cent in 1970.

One effect of such changes has been the weakening of social stratification. This was reflected in a study of the social origins of present elites published by Warner and Abegglen in 1955. Their

---

[8] Theodore Schultze, *The Economic Value of Education* (New York: Columbia University Press, 1963); Frederick Harbison and Charles A. Myers, *Education, Manpower, and Economic Growth* (New York: McGraw-Hill Book Company, 1963).

[9] *National Education Association Research Bulletin,* XXXIX, 3 (October 1961).

data showed both an "openness in the occupational and status structure" that contrasted with Warner's earlier concern about "blocked
mobility," and the importance of higher education as the basis of
upward mobility. For instance, about twice as many business leaders were college graduates in 1955 as were in 1928.

> Today's mobility in business and in government—and, for that
> matter, in all the higher professions and all the highly regarded oc-
> cupations—is primarily by higher education. It is not only the royal
> road but perhaps the only road to success for the vast majority.[10]

The problem of the unskilled.   Conversely, the prospects are
gloomy for youths who do not attend college, and particularly bad
for those who fail to complete high school. According to Daniel
Schreiber, Director of the National Education Association Project
on School Dropouts, thirty years ago two out of three sixth-grade
pupils did not go on to receive a high school diploma whereas today
only one out of three drops out before graduation. The decline in
unskilled "entry" jobs for young people, and the higher educational
requirements posed for many positions, are the key to the paradox
that as schools have increased their holding power, the dropout
problem has become more serious. The greatest amount of unemployment is among young people who, though constituting less than
10 per cent of the labor force, account for almost 20 per cent of the
unemployed. A U.S. Labor Department survey showed the jobless
rate of 1962 dropouts to be about twice as high as that of high school
graduates. Approximately 1 million youngsters who reached the age
of eighteen in 1960 had already dropped out of school; of the 26
million young workers entering the work force during the 1960's,
an estimated 7.5 million will lack a high school education.

Michael notes the special impact of cybernation on dock, factory,
and mine operations that have in the past provided Negroes with
their steadiest employment. Constituting 10 per cent of the working
force, Negroes account for 20 per cent of the unemployed. On the
basis of her study of the work situation of youth in New York City,[11]
Mary Conway Kohler relates that not a single graduate of the electrical wiring course in a predominantly Negro high school in Wash-

---

[10] W. Lloyd Warner, *American Life, Dream and Reality* (Chicago: The University of Chicago Press, 1962), p. 152.

[11] *Youth and Work in New York City,* directed by Mary Conway Kohler, as-
sisted by Marcia Freedman (New York: Taconic Foundation, n.d.).

ington, D.C., got a job in that field, although 80 per cent of the white students who had taken the same course in another school did. In 1964, according to a U.S. Labor Department report, unemployment rates among Negro teen-agers were 23 per cent for boys, 31 per cent for girls.

In these circumstances, two additional responsibilities have been suggested for the schools. Noting with deep alarm the unemployment rate among youth, particularly in the Negro slum areas of large cities, and finding effective placement agencies in only a few cities, Conant recommends that school guidance officers, especially in large cities, be given the responsibility for following the post-high school careers of youth from the time they leave school until they are twenty-one.[12] Both the National Education Association's Educational Policies Commission and Secretary of Labor Willard Wirtz have recommended that two years of free public education beyond the high school be provided for all youths. Whether the two years should be devoted to additional general education (as suggested by the Commission[13]) or to technical vocational training (as proposed by Secretary Wirtz), the recommendation to raise the compulsory education age to eighteen suggests the increasingly rigorous demands of the economy upon the school.

Vocational Education

The issue of the system of vocational education in the high schools today was raised anew by Conant's recommendation that the secondary school curriculum provide programs for the development of "marketable skills," either as electives in the comprehensive high school or in separate vocational and technical schools.[14] The federal assistance provided first by the Smith-Hughes Act of 1917 and later by the George-Barden Act of 1946 has made available to the states, on a matching basis, about 25 million dollars annually for financing the training and salaries of teachers in trade and industrial occupa-

---

[12] James Bryant Conant, *Slums and Suburbs* (New York: McGraw-Hill Book Company, 1961), p. 41. By permission of Educational Testing Service, Princeton, New Jersey.

[13] *Universal Opportunity for Education Beyond the High Schools* (Washington, D.C.: National Education Association, 1964).

[14] James Bryant Conant, *The American High School Today* (New York: McGraw-Hill Book Company, 1959).

tions, agriculture, home economics, and distributive occupations. In view of the precipitous decline of job opportunities in agriculture, the fact that a sizable portion of the money has gone to this area of study has been used as evidence of the lack of realism in the program. In Judge Kohler's opinion, much vocational schooling has little relation to the real world of work because of obsolete equipment and the failure on the part of schools, industry, and unions to agree on the appropriate training for various occupations. The drop-out rate in vocational high schools in New York City, in fact, is higher than that in academic high schools: less than 38 per cent of the students in vocational high school graduate, as compared with 62 per cent of those in the academic high schools. According to Judge Kohler:

> It is extremely questionable and certainly never has been demonstrated whether the training absorbed by vocational high school graduates is useful to them in getting employment and advancing on the job. It is doubtful whether the enormous investment in the vocational schools and the high cost of instruction is bringing the expected return.[15]

The responsibility of the schools. Proponents of vocational education have argued that public schools have an obligation to provide for the development of manual skills as well as intellectual skills, that occupational training capitalizes on the interests of many students for whom school would otherwise be unattractive, and—in the absence of an adequate apprenticeship system—provides skilled workers badly needed by the economy.[16] Present legislation, however, is based on the premise that the best education for vocational students is that which provides training in the skills and knowledge of a specific occupation, and even vocational educators grant that the full-time school is not the ideal place for producing fully skilled workers. Other educators deny that the secondary schools could prepare students for the thousands of specific jobs that exist in the modern American economy—or that they should: "the young person would be prepared for his first job—but not for a working career."[17] With advances made possible by modern tech-

---

[15] *Youth and Work in New York City, op. cit.,* p. 12.
[16] Henry David (ed.), *Education and Manpower* (New York: Columbia University Press, 1960), pp. 145–47.
[17] *Ibid.,* pp. 74, 144.

nology, the obsolescence of skills will be greatly accelerated; it has been estimated that, during the next century, at least one of every two members of the labor force may need to learn a new vocation twice during his lifetime.

Vocational education in the form of training for specific skills has also been condemned as "class education" and undemocratic. Critics point to the inferiority of the nonvocational courses taken by vocational students as compared with those courses available to other students, and to the fact that the vocational student is excluded from admission to college. Mortimer Adler has attacked Conant's advocacy of education for "marketable skills" for all students except the approximately 15 per cent of the academically talented as "unashamedly undemocratic, or worse—antidemocratic." Arthur Bestor has attacked vocational training, along with " 'life adjustment' education, the study of contemporary problems" and "a concern with immediate everyday experience" as a "hopelessly inadequate scheme of education for a changing world." A program of science, mathematics, history, and language—in other words, a liberal education —is, Bestor argues, the only adequate preparation for coping with a world in which "everyone belongs to the governing class" and virtually every occupation has become "intellectualized." The school, he insists, cannot offer training on the job; its function is "to provide training for the job—in other words, training in the intellectual processes that now underlie all jobs."[18]

Communications, Culture, and the School

The role of mass media.   Of all aspects of contemporary life that have been affected by the revolution in technology, developments in communication have been of utmost importance to the culture in general and to the schools in particular. Only in recent decades has technology made possible the mass media by which information can be transmitted to an infinitely large audience simultaneously.[19] Schramm believes the contemporary communications

---

[18] Arthur Bestor, "The Education Really Needed for a Changing World," *Harvard Educational Review* XXVII (Winter 1957), 1–8.

[19] Franklin Fearing, "Social Impact of the Mass Media of Communication," in *Mass Media and Education,* edited by Nelson B. Henry, Fifty-third Yearbook of the National Society for the Study of Education, (Chicago: The University of Chicago Press, 1954), p. 166.

media are distinguished from those of a half-century ago by their "extraordinary pervasiveness," judged by the amount of time they command from both adults and children.[20] In addition, the very nature of radio and particularly television means that experiences of incredible variety and vividness are available to children that could not be provided through the printed word alone.

The mass media have contributed to the development of a more homogeneous culture by allowing the wide diffusion of common standards, images, information, opinions, and "models" of behavior and speech. Ordinarily, it is the negative effect of such diffusion that is stressed, but the unifying effect of common experiences in a country as large as the United States can, of course, have a positive value as well. The criticism is directed toward the low standards that seem inherent in media seeking to appeal to a universal audience, so the criterion of quality becomes that of the "average" reader, listener, and viewer. The amount of violence and brutality purveyed by television programs has been a matter of major concern. There are those who believe such programs are directly responsible for increased juvenile crime and violence through imitation and suggestion; others point out that the impact of communication is a function not only of the content of the message but also of the need-value-belief system of the interpreter and the situation in which his reaction occurs.[21] Teachers, Schramm suggests, should be alert for signs of maladjustment—withdrawal or aggressiveness, for example —associated with the heavy use of television, but remarks that such symptoms are not caused by television: "They grow out of personal, home, or peer group inadequacies. But they are the kind of fire that television feeds."[22]

Mass media in the school. Experimentation with the use of mass media in the schools has been stimulated by the rise in enrollments and the shortage of teachers. Educators have also been interested in studying the effects of commercial television on the knowledge and attitudes of children as these affect school instruction. Schramm and Parker have found that television gives children, par-

---

[20] Wilbur Schramm, "Mass Media and Educational Policy," in *Social Forces Affecting American Education,* edited by Nelson B. Henry, Sixtieth Yearbook of the National Society for the Study of Education (Chicago: The University of Chicago Press, 1961), pp. 207–28.

[21] Fearing, *op. cit.,* pp. 170–76.

[22] Schramm, *op. cit.,* p. 216.

ticularly the brightest and the slowest, a "faster start" by sending them into first grade with larger recognition vocabularies than are possessed by children without television experience, although the advantage disappears in a few years. Exposure to adult material contributes to a kind of "immature maturity" on the part of the child. Television provides more knowledge about the fantasy world—the world of entertainment—than about the real world; hence it encourages withdrawal from, rather than à direct attack upon, current problems. These investigators concluded that television's greatest challenge to the schools consists in its vividness of imagery and "constantly rising curve of excitement" that provides a standard against which the child judges his other experiences, including those in the classroom.[23]

Technology and Value Changes

The emergent values.   Since the end of World War II, interest has focused upon the implications of economic and technological change for the dominant value system in America and, hence, in the schools. Riesman supplied the vocabulary with which much of the discussion was carried on, contrasting the "inner-directedness" of the "old" middle class (bankers, entrepreneurs) with the "other-directedness" of the "new" middle class (bureaucrats, salaried employees). The shift from a high valuation on achievement to a desire for group acceptance has been linked with the growing influence of the mass media and the peer group. In Riesman's vivid metaphor, the control equipment of the other-directed individual resembles radar; the inner-directed man's control equipment resembles a gyroscope.[24] Part of the evidence for the changing values of the urban middle class was provided by a series of studies of child-training practices conducted in Boston, California, and Detroit. These studies appeared to show that middle-class parents were no longer more rigorous than lower-class parents in their training of children for feeding and cleanliness habits and the control of impulses and desires. It also appeared, however, that middle-class parents still had

---

[23] *Ibid.,* pp. 210ff.
[24] David Riesman, with Nathan Glazer and Reuel Denney, *The Lonely Crowd* (New Haven: Yale University Press, 1950).

higher expectations for the child, including his progress in school, than did lower-class parents.[25] From the anthropologists came evidence that traditional middle-class values (puritan morality, work-success ethic, individualism, achievement) were giving way to the emergent values of sociability, relativistic morality, consideration for others, hedonistic present-time orientation, and conformity.[26] According to Clyde Kluckhohn, who provides the most comprehensive survey of the evidence for changes in American values, "the most generally agreed upon, the best documented, and the most pervasive value shift," is the decline of the "Protestant ethic." Strictly personal values have receded in importance at the expense of more publicly standardized "group values," whether they are those of an organization, a community, a social class, a profession, a minority, or an interest group.[27]

Spindler is convinced that the culture of professional education has a clear bias toward an "emergent-oriented ethos," although there will be conflicts within individuals, particularly teachers who—drawn from the tradition-oriented lower-middle classes—must make their adaptation to the emergent values of schools of education. Lipset, who is critical of the Riesman thesis because he believes that both the equalitarian and achievement ethics have always been part of the American tradition, suggests a pendulum effect: an emphasis which shifts from one value to the other, depending upon social and economic circumstances. Thus, in the depression and New Deal of the 1930's, equalitarianism was uppermost; in the more conservative and prosperous 1950's, achievement became important. Lipset identifies progressive education with the supremacy of equalitarian values and liberal politics in the 1930's, and cites the opposition on the part of educators (and progressives) to providing special encouragement to the gifted child and their criticism of special schools

---

25 Urie Bronfenbrenner, "Socialization and Social Class Through Time and Space," in *Readings in Social Psychology,* edited by Eleanor E. Maccoby, Theodore M. Newcomb, and Eugene L. Hartley (New York: Holt, Rinehart & Winston, Inc., 1958), pp. 400–25.

26 George D. Spindler, "Education in a Transforming American Culture," in *Education and Culture,* edited by George D. Spindler (New York: Holt, Rinehart & Winston, Inc., 1963), pp. 132–47.

27 Clyde Kluckhohn, "Have There Been Discernible Shifts in American Values During the Past Generation?" in *The American Style,* edited by Elton E. Morison (New York: Harper & Row, Publishers, 1958), pp. 184, 204.

for talented children as "undemocratic" in conferring special privileges on a minority.[28]

The progressive teacher, as Riesman describes him, is more interested in "the child's social and psychological adjustment than with his academic performance," and scans the intellectual performance "for signs of social maladjustment." For such teachers, he says, not the intellectual content of what is taught but the adjustment of children in the group is the important thing:

> ... the children are supposed to learn democracy by underplaying the skills of intellect and overplaying the skills of gregariousness and amiability—skill democracy, in fact, based on respect for ability to do something, tends to survive only in athletics.[29]

Elsewhere, however, Riesman grants that the progressive reformers wished, not to "dilute the intellectuality of the schools, but to encourage a less narrow and doctrinaire intellectuality, and to add to it." He recognizes "the dilemmas of democratic education," which he doubts could be "willed away if only one could restore the classical curriculum, and discover an elite to administer and another to endure it." He argues, however, that society today provides ample opportunity for the development of that social maturity upon which progressive education put such emphasis. In "countercyclical" fashion, the schools need now to provide "protection for certain long-term intellectual and humanistic interests that are momentarily under pressure and apt to be squeezed out."[30]

The stress on education.   In opposition to Riesman's original thesis, Parsons and White have argued that a highly complex economy demands higher competence and, hence, an upgrading of education for the technical proficiencies and decision-making abilities that will enable a society to work and to preserve itself in the international competition.[31] This point of view is implicit in the pressure exerted on the school in the last decade for a thorough renovation

---

[28] Seymour Lipset, "A Changing American Character?" in *Culture and Social Character; The Work of David Riesman Reviewed,* edited by Seymour Lipset and Leo Lowenthal (New York: The Free Press of Glencoe, Inc., 1961), pp. 136–71.

[29] Riesman, *op. cit.,* pp. 80, 84.

[30] David Riesman, *Constraint and Variety in American Education* (Garden City, N.Y.: Doubleday & Company, Inc., 1958), especially pp. 142–51. Reprinted by permission of the University of Nebraska Press, Lincoln 8, Nebraska.

[31] Talcott Parsons and Winston White, "The Link Between Character and Society," in *Culture and Social Character . . . , op. cit.,* pp. 89–135, particularly pp. 110–11.

of curriculum (particularly in mathematics, foreign languages, and science) and the development of various special provisions for the academically talented.

It has already been pointed out that the same economic changes that have made these devices necessary have aggravated the problem of the student with less academic talent. As a consequence, demands are made upon the school that can be synthesized only with great difficulty. To a Bestor, the school's most important responsibility is the education of the gifted child, and the changed character of the school population is irrelevant to that task; whatever proportion of the school population gifted children may represent, their needs must be met. It is only in the "demented" view of the "educationist" that such children are defined as exceptional: correctly viewed, the gifted child should set the pace for the school; the curriculum for the average child is the one that is "derivative."[32] On the other hand, those concerned with the less talented student, and particularly with the integration of minority-group children, believe homogeneous grouping reinstitutes segregation within desegregated schools, and harms the social and emotional development of children. They are willing, if Martin Deutsch speaks for them, to accept some unfairness to the majority-group child, if that is what results from heterogeneous grouping, as "simply the price that must now be paid for one hundred years of segregation and lack of attention to the special educational problems of the minority child."[33] Another attack is led by Paul Goodman, who vigorously assails both those who see the salvation of underprivileged children in "more schooling of the middle-class variety" and those who believe society will be lost without more rigorous intellectual standards in the school. Goodman attacks the assumption that extended schooling is the only means by which all young people should be prepared for their careers, and denounces the present academic system as harmful to every kind of youth: humiliating to the slow, anxiety-producing for the average, and ruinous to the authentically scholarly who,

---

[32] Arthur Bestor, "Educating the Gifted Child," *New Republic,* CXXXVI (March 4, 1957), 12–16.

[33] Martin Deutsch, "Dimensions of the School's Role in the Problems of Integration," in *Integrating the Urban School,* edited by Gordon J. Klopf and Israel A. Laster (New York: Teacher's College, Bureau of Publications, Columbia University, 1963), pp. 37–38.

"bribed and pampered . . . forget the meaning of their gifts." Our best brains, Goodman claims, should be trying to devise

> . . . various means of educating and paths of growing up, appropriate to various talents, conditions, and careers. We should be experimenting with different kinds of school, no school at all, the real city as school, farm schools, practical apprenticeships, guided travel, work camps, little theaters and local newspapers, community service. . . . Probably more than anything, we need a community, and community spirit, in which many adults who know something, and not only professional teachers, will pay attention to the young.[34]

John Gardner has urged that both high morale throughout the society and the "richly varied potentialities of mankind" require recognition of many kinds of excellence at many levels. If our conception of excellence is not applied "to every degree of ability and to every socially acceptable activity," he believes, we will not get the "almost universal striving for good performance" upon which depend the "tone and fiber of our society."[35] Whether or not Gardner's viewpoint gives the conception of excellence sufficient meaning, it probably will not diminish the partisanship for specific types of excellence that will continue to provide contradictory pressures upon the public school and its program.

---

[34] Paul Goodman, *Compulsory Mis-Education* (New York: Horizon Press, 1964), pp. 173–74, 181.

[35] John W. Gardner, *Excellence: Can We Be Equal and Excellent Too?* (New York: Harper & Row, Publishers, 1961), pp. 131, 132.

CHAPTER V

The School in the Metropolitan Community

The community school movement focused attention upon the powerful effects of the community upon the child—effects that could be called *educative* in the sense of being formative, whether for good or ill. Hart writes:

> ... [The community] gives most of its children their eventual attitudes about work; about money-making; about gambling; about law and respect for laws; about respect for persons; about moral relationships; about responsibility; about "getting away with things."[1]

Conant's study of schools in the city slums convinced him that "the nature of the community largely determines what goes on in the school. . . . [T]he community and the school are inseparable."[2] Clearly, the "education" given by the community may be largely for ill rather than for good; indeed, community school enthusiasts have made the contrast between standards in the school and those in the community the basis, in part, for the demand that the curriculum be organized around community problems. Whether or not it is either appropriate or possible for schools to undertake community improvement, the characteristics of the community that are resources or obstacles to the goals of the schools are facts of which educators must take account.

The Process of Metropolitanization

Urban growth. The dominant pattern of community living in America has changed from agrarian to urban to metropolitan. The percentage of population living in urban areas has increased steadily since the first census in 1790, reflecting the industrialization which created the cities and made them the major sources of em-

---

[1] Joseph K. Hart, *Adult Education* (New York: Thomas Y. Crowell Company, 1927), p. 86.

[2] James Bryant Conant, *Slums and Suburbs* (New York: McGraw-Hill Book Company, 1961), p. 20. Reprinted by permission of Educational Testing Service, Princeton, N.J.

ployment and opportunity in America. Outmigration reduced the farm population by an estimated one fifth in the 1920's, by one eighth during the 1930's, and by nearly one third in the 1940's. The same pattern was evident in the 1950's, and the rural farm population is expected to continue to decline, both in actual numbers and in relation to total population.[3]

Schnore[4] describes urban centers at the turn of the century as compact and self-contained entities, the residents of which lived near their places of work, in tenements and row houses. Only the wealthier members of the community could live outside the city and travel to their places of business by automobile or by interurban railway. Although subcenters appeared along railroad lines, they were largely independent of the central city. Larger urban centers grew more rapidly than smaller ones, mainly because of the immigrants that were admitted to this country between 1900 and 1920. World War I marked the end of large-scale immigration, which meant that urban factories had to attract workers from rural areas to meet the wartime demand for labor.

The decentralization of industry. The decentralization of industry that began in the 1920's was the result of several factors: cheap electrical power, the telephone, the automobile, and the lower cost of land in the rural "ring" surrounding the city. As a consequence, the urban subcenters that appeared in increasing numbers grew more rapidly than the center. They also began to lose their independence: the process of metropolitanization was underway. More than 60 per cent of the population now lives in 212 standard metropolitan areas; by 1980, nearly 80 per cent will be living in such areas. As suburbs and developments spread out and meet, the pattern of living becomes that of the "megalopolis," already exemplified on the East and West Coasts and expected to be repeated at various points throughout the country.

---

[3] Eleanor H. Bernert and Charles B. Nam, "Demographic Factors Affecting American Education," in *Social Forces Affecting American Education,* edited by Nelson B. Henry, Sixtieth Yearbook of the National Society for the Study of Education (Chicago: The University of Chicago Press, 1961), pp. 100–101.

[4] Leo F. Schnore, "Metropolitan Growth and Decentralization," in *The Suburban Community,* edited by William Dobriner (New York: G. P. Putnam's Sons, 1958), pp. 3–20.

The Community

Family, school, and society.   In sociological terms, America has been transformed from a folk or *Gemeinschaft* society in which primary-group relationships, limited differentiation of roles, and tradition predominate, to an associational or *Gesellschaft* society characterized by secondary-group relationships, segmented roles (each of which involves only part of the personality), and the substitution of law and contract for tradition as modes of social control.[5] One consequence of fundamental significance to the school has been the shift from the extended family that was a unit of economic production to the nuclear family of parents and children that is based on companionship, consensus, democratic family relationships, and the personal happiness of family members.[6] At the other extreme, there is what Kimball and McClelland refer to as the "world of the great superstructures"—the corporate activities of industry, finance, government, transportation, and the like, through which order is achieved within a professionalized and specialized community.[7]

Kimball and McClelland's treatment of the function of education rests basically upon the resulting "social and cultural dichotomy" that now exists between the private and public sectors. "Domesticity and community," unified in agrarian society, have been separated, and consequently the individual no longer can establish a meaningful relation to his society on the basis of his personal experience; he cannot merely extend, so to speak, the features of his private world to the great "superstructures." The school becomes a transitional institution, for it is by the process of education that the young are

[5] Ely Chinoy, *Sociological Perspective* (New York: Random House, 1954), pp. 31–34.

[6] Ernest W. Burgess, "The Family in a Changing Society," *American Journal of Sociology,* LIII (May 1948), 417–22.

[7] Solon T. Kimball and James E. McClelland, Jr., *Education and the New America* (New York: Random House, 1962), pp. 34–36. See also Scott Greer, "Order and Change in Metropolitan Society, " in *Education in Urban Society,* edited by B. J. Chandler, L. J. Stiles, and John I. Kitsuse (New York: Dodd, Mead & Co., 1962), Chap. 2; and Talcott Parsons and Winston White, "The Link Between Character and Society," in *Culture and Social Character: The Work of David Riesman Reviewed,* edited by Seymour Lipset and Leo Lowenthal (New York: The Free Press of Glencoe, Inc., 1961), p. 109, the remarks on the "quantitative expansion" of the occupational system through the increasing proportion of the working population in economic roles structurally segregated from nonoccupational contexts, particularly those of kinship (e.g., the family farm).

gradually separated from family and locality and are prepared to "join the great corporate systems and to establish their own independent nuclear families." This demands a "peculiarly intellectual conception of education": in the agrarian society, the relation between the individual and his social world is "direct and experienced," in metropolitan culture, the relation is "indirect rather than direct, cognitive rather than emotive, partially rather than fully participative, symbolically constructed rather than historically experienced."[8] To perform its transitional function properly, therefore, the school must teach the disciplines of logic and mathematics, experimentation, natural history, and aesthetic form, for these are the disciplines of the public world, not merely academic studies. Such disciplines, Kimball and McClelland assert, are

> ... the primordial rules of thought that guide our most fundamental interpretations of the world, ... the substitutes in the contemporary world for the gossip and sorcery of primitive village life, ... institutionally legitimate modes of social control.[9]

This thesis again presents the demand for intellectualizing the school curriculum, as the indispensable means by which both a rationalized impersonal metropolitan culture may be sustained and the individual may escape alienation from—or (in the terminology of these authors) achieve commitment within—a corporate society. At the same time, however, the metropolis as an environment for education reveals features which make it increasingly difficult for schools to fulfill such responsibilities or even to perform the simpler tasks undertaken in an earlier era. The city is in deep trouble, in which its schools are inevitably implicated.

The uneven rate of growth between central cities and the suburbs has continued. Between 1950 and 1960, the central cities grew only slightly—by some 4 million, or 8.2 per cent—and some even lost population. During this period the suburbs gained more than 17 million, a 47.2 per cent increase. It has been estimated that, by 1975, the central cities will have 12 million more people, the suburban ring 54 million more—32 million in open country or unincorporated areas (exurbia), and 21 million in areas incorporated within

---

[8] Kimball and McClelland, *op. cit.,* p. 284, 303.
[9] *Ibid.,* pp. 303–304.

the suburban ring.[10] One consequence of this pattern is the creation of homogeneous communities that tend to rigidify the social-class structure and to complicate the attempts of the school to perform its traditional function as an agent of social unification. Havighurst distinguishes three types of communities that are being created within the metropolis: upper-middle-class and upper-class suburbs, with a very small number of lower-middle-class residents; working-class and lower-middle-class suburbs—the "common-man" variety —with very few lower-lower-class residents; and the city slums, made up almost entirely of lower-class people, as many as half of whom will be lower-lower-class.[11] The process has been described more succinctly as one of "ever-increasing stratification, making the cities the abode of the very poor and the very rich, with the middle class living in the suburbs."[12]

Flight to the suburbs. One of the important reasons for the flight to the suburbs on the part of the middle class, as both Slayton and Havighurst point out, is the belief that the suburbs offer oppor- tunities for better education. The schools are crucial elements, there- fore, in attempts to preserve the self-contained city. Havighurst suggests that the "ethos" of a school can be expressed quantitatively in a "status ratio" formulated as $[2\ (U + UM) + LM] \div [UL + 2LL]$. The number of upper-class and upper-middle-class pupils is weighted twice as heavily as the number of lower-middle-class chil- dren because the former are

> ... about twice as likely to go to college and to exhibit other forms of academic interest and achievement as youth from the lower-middle class ... while youth from the lower-lower class are only about half as likely as pupils from the upper-lower class to show these characteristics.[13]

When this ratio drops below a certain point, middle-class parents move out of the neighborhood or put their children into private

---

[10] Jessie Barnard, *American Community Behavior* (New York: Holt, Rinehart & Winston, Inc., 1962), p. 125.

[11] Robert J. Havighurst, "Social Class Influences on American Education," in *Social Forces Affecting American Education, op. cit.,* pp. 139–40.

[12] William L. Slayton, "The Influence of Urban Renewal on Education," *School Life,* XLIV (June 1962), 9–12.

[13] Robert J. Havighurst, "Metropolitan Development and the Educational Sys- tem," *The School Review,* LXIX (Autumn 1961), 251–67. Reprinted by per- mission of The University of Chicago Press.

schools. Slayton therefore emphasizes that the success of urban renewal depends, in large part, upon the development of school programs that provide the kind of educational opportunity demanded by middle- and upper-class families, and that also is aligned to support efforts to redevelop slum areas.

Deterioration of the central city. "Everywhere the center decays, the peripheries boom."[14] Paradoxically, activities of the federal government aimed at solving urban problems—traffic and housing, for example—have contributed to the deterioration of the · central city.[15] When property is removed from the tax rolls and condemned for the construction of freeways and traffic arteries, the lost revenue cannot be recovered. In the case of housing projects, the annual payment in lieu of taxes often is available to the schools only after a considerable lapse of time, and may be less than the schools received in taxes from properties that housed a much smaller pupil population. As tenants replace homeowners, real property deteriorates and this, added to the aging of property, has resulted in a decrease of property valuations per pupil. In addition, state legislatures—which have a controlling voice in the city's fiscal affairs—are often apportioned in favor of rural areas: thus Denver has received $2.3 million a year in state aid for a school system of 90,000 children while an adjacent semirural county with 18,000 pupils has received $2.4 million.[16] Consequently, the U.S. Supreme Court decisions in 1964 regarding apportionment may have a greater impact on the schools than its decisions dealing directly with educational issues.

Deterioration of the central city has resulted in contrasts between its schools and those of wealthy suburban communities with respect to expenditures per pupil, quality of buildings and equipment, and size of professional staff. These contrasts represent important inequities in educational opportunities. Conditions in metropolitan areas have created difficult problems in recruiting a sufficient number of teachers to staff city schools. The result is that the cities must

---

14 Greer, *op. cit.,* p. 40.

15 U.S. Office of Education, *The Impact of Urbanization on Education,* Summary Report of a Conference May 28–29, 1962 (Washington, D.C.: USGPO, 1962), p. 3.

16 Seymour Freedgood, "New Strength in City Hall," in *Exploding Metropolis,* edited by the Editors of *Fortune* (Garden City, N.Y.: Doubleday & Company, Inc., 1957, 1958), p. 64.

employ teachers with emergency, substandard, or temporary credentials. For instance, in New York City, according to Pillard,[17] between one fourth and one third of all teachers now in the classrooms are substitutes. Big-city schools, from elementary through senior high, have consistently shown the highest pupil-to-teacher ratios, and the salary advantage once enjoyed by the largest urban districts has almost disappeared.

Those who have moved to the suburbs have been replaced in the central city by the "new" minority groups: Negro and white Southern migrants, Mexican-Americans, and Puerto Ricans. Of the approximately 800,000 Puerto Ricans in the United States, 600,000 are in New York City. In addition to the language problem, they have the disadvantage of racial ambiguity. Darker of skin than most American citizens, about two thirds of the Puerto Ricans are classified as Negro, but only about one third of them were so classified at home.[18] The racial attitudes encountered in the new land are therefore a source, not only of deep resentment, but of bewilderment.[19] Riesman mentions Puerto Rican children have refused to learn to speak English because they felt that, if they did, they might be taken for Negroes.

Both Appalachian whites, or "Okies," and Negroes are representatives of a rural culture that presents problems of assimilation in a metropolitan environment. The Negro belongs to a recently urbanized minority. As late as 1900, over 80 per cent of all Negroes in the United States lived in rural areas—90 per cent of them in the South; by 1960, 73 per cent were urban dwellers, and outside of the South over 90 per cent lived in cities.[20] The curtailment of immigration after World War I, and the industrial developments during and after World War II, attracted millions of Southern Negroes to the North, Midwest, and West, so that the proportion of Northern Negroes to all Negroes in the United States increased from 13 per cent

[17] Matthew J. Pillard, "Teachers for Urban Schools," in *Education in Urban Society, op. cit.,* pp. 196–98.

[18] Henry Miller, "New York City's Puerto Rican Pupils: A Problem of Acculturation," *School and Society,* LXXVI (August 30, 1952), 129–32; and Oscar Handlin, *The Newcomers* (Cambridge, Mass.: Harvard University Press, 1959), p. 59.

[19] See Joseph Monserrat, "School Integration: A Puerto Rican View," in *Integrating the Urban School,* edited by Gordon J. Klopf and Israel A. Laster (New York: Teachers College, Bureau of Publications, Columbia University, 1963), pp. 45–60.

[20] Raymond W. Mack, "The Changing Ethnic Fabric of the Metropolis," in *Education in Urban Society, op. cit.,* p. 61.

in 1920 to 39 per cent in 1960.[21] The shift in Negro population from the South amounted to nearly 1.5 million in the 1950's—almost a quarter of a million more than in the 1940's. Of the 18.8 million Negroes in the United States in 1960, over 6 million lived in the twenty-five largest cities, making up 19.7 per cent of the total population of those cities. In only two of the five largest cities (New York and Los Angeles) do the nonwhite voting-age groups constitute less than 20 per cent of the population. In the forty-year period 1920–60, the proportion of Negroes to the total population of cities having 50,000 or more Negroes in 1960 rose from 4.1 per cent to 21.1 per cent.[22]

The Impact on Education

The new slums.   A spirit of hopelessness and alienation has been said to characterize the slum dweller of today, in contrast with the spirit of hope that marked the white European immigrant who inhabited the slums of the late nineteenth and early twentieth centuries. The European immigrant was encouraged by the example of others like him who had worked their way out of poverty, and the shortage of unskilled labor in an expanding economy provided a solid basis for that hope. Also, he was sustained by a native culture that gave him stability and direction.[23] Today, the racial minorities —particularly the Negro, but the Mexican and Puerto Rican as well —suffer under the double impact of racial discrimination and the general unemployment caused by automation. Housing discrimination has established a de facto segregation of education in the North to match the de jure segregation in the South. Under slum conditions, the task of the school becomes well-nigh impossible and, in turn, inferior schools reinforce slum conditions.

Although the Supreme Court's desegregation decision of 1954 made plain the status of de jure segregation, it left untouched the question of de facto segregation. For example, one elementary school in New Rochelle, New York, had become predominantly Negro because the school board in 1930 had redrawn the school district

---

[21] *Public School Segregation and Integration in the North* (Washington, D.C.: National Association of Intergroup Relations Officials, 1963), p. 5.

[22] *Ibid.,* Table I, p. 6.

[23] Conant, *op. cit.,* p. 37; Michael Harrington, *The Other America: Poverty in the United States* (New York: The Macmillan Company, 1962).

lines to match the Negro residential area. In 1961 a U.S. District Court declared that such gerrymandering violated the Fourteenth Amendment. There has been no final ruling on the constitutionality of segregation not resulting from official action of school authorities. In 1964 and 1965, U.S. Circuit Court decisions have allowed de facto segregation in the Gary, Indiana, and Kansas City, Kansas, school systems, but also allowed the New York City School Board to take action to minimize such segregation in a Brooklyn area; and in each case the U.S. Supreme Court has refused to review the decision. Yet the paradox of proscribing segregation based on official action while failing to provide a remedy for segregation arising out of other factors has raised a question on which the U.S. Supreme Court ultimately may be forced to decide. The U.S. Commission on Civil Rights has interpreted the decision in *Taylor* v. *Board of Education of New Rochelle* as a warning that

> ... school boards having uniracial schools can no longer justify it merely on the basis of residential patterns in combination with a neigborhood school policy. Any existing segregation may be constitutionally suspect. School boards that want to operate their schools in a constitutional manner may have to inquire into the cause of any existing segregation. They may have to prove that zoning lines follow residential patterns by coincidence, not design; that the sites and sizes of schools were not fixed to assure segregation; that racial residential patterns were not officially created in the first instance.[24]

In any event, the principle that separate educational facilities are inherently unequal was clear enough in the May 1954 decision. That decision presented a straightforward challenge to educational authorities who wish to fulfill the responsibility of the public school system—that of providing equal educational opportunity to all children—and formed the basis on which an aroused Negro leadership could exert pressure for action on the white community. Such action has taken two main forms: the devising of techniques for desegregating minority-group schools, and the development of compensatory programs for the culturally deprived youth of the slums.[25]

---

[24] *Education,* 1961 Commission on Civil Rights Report, Book 2 (Washington, D.C.: USGPO, 1961), p. 174.

[25] For detailed discussion of these categories, see Frederick Shaw, "Educating Culturally Deprived Youth in Urban Centers," *Phi Delta Kappan,* XLV (November, 1963), pp. 91–7; *Public School Segregation and Integration in the North, op. cit.,* pp. 53–66.

Desegregation programs.   One means of desegregating minority-group schools has been the addition of racial balance to the criteria for choosing the site of new schools. District lines have been redrawn to take account of the ethnic composition of the area from which the school draws its students. A special form of this rezoning is the Princeton Plan, in which two formerly separate districts that served predominantly white and predominantly minority-group pupils, respectively, are consolidated into one attendance district; all students in the district attend one school for certain grades (K-3, for example), and the other school for the remaining grades. Communities with one minority-group school have dispersed its students among other schools and either closed the unused building or converted it to other use. Some cities have systematized the transfer privilege; under the name of *open enrollment,* for example, New York City permits the transfer of white and minority-group pupils from predominantly Negro or Puerto Rican "sending" schools to underutilized "receiving" schools in other districts.

Some of these measures, as in the case of the open-enrollment plan, move children into desegregated schools but clearly do not desegregate the "sending" schools; this could be done only by reverse transfer, which meets strong opposition from white parents whose children are to be transferred. Other devices are applicable mainly in smaller cities; a significant change in the school situation of a large slum area may be impossible without a drastic alteration in the community housing pattern, as Niemeyer has admitted must be the case in the schools of New York's Harlem.[26] In Washington, D.C., the loss of white students by migration to the suburbs or transfer to private schools has resulted in a school population that, in 1962, was over 80 per cent Negro. In many cases, then, the only alternative is to attempt to upgrade the quality of education of the segregated school itself. Some oppose such a policy as a return to the separate-but-equal doctrine; others favor it as a means of facilitating the integration of minority-group children transferred to white schools and reducing the opposition to reverse transfer.

The programs that have been developed have called, not merely for equalization, but for additional services and attention to compensate for the special disabilities of the slum child. Of these pro-

26 John A. Niemeyer, "School Integration: The School's Responsibility," in *Integrating the Urban School, op. cit.,* p. 68.

grams, the best-known are Higher Horizons in New York City, and the Great Cities Grey Areas School Improvement Programs involving fourteen cities in the Northeast, the Midwest, the West, and the border states. With access to more money than the normal school budget would provide, both programs have used small classes, special consultants, and increased counselling services. They have given particular attention to reading deficiencies, and have employed both individual and group counselling to help identify personal problems that interfere with learning and to provide students with information about occupations and higher education. Attention has also been devoted to raising the aspirational level of students, to convince them of the value and relevance of education to their lives. Higher Horizons has taken its students into the community—to concerts, museums, theaters, industrial plants, and colleges—as a means of expanding the scope of their experience and enhancing their motivation. Afterschool and evening programs oriented to community needs have been offered, and schools participating in these programs have worked with parents, helping them to appreciate and understand the value of education for their children, and also helping the parents themselves.

The Higher Horizons Program (originally the Demonstration Guidance Project) began with three junior high school grades and continued through the senior high schools attended by the students originally participating in the project. Later, the program was extended downward to the elementary school. The Grey Areas School Improvement Program has operated from elementary through senior high school. Martin Deutsch, Director of the Institute of Developmental Studies of New York Medical College, has begun an experiment in nursery education for Negro and white slum children in ten New York City public schools and five day-care centers. This experiment assumes that the schools, if they are to offset the poverty of experience of slum children, must begin working with them at the age of three or four, in order to develop the verbal and perceptual skills that are taken for granted in the first grade and are acquired as a matter of course by middle-class children.[27]

---

[27] Charles E. Silberman, "Give Slum Children a Chance," *Harper's Magazine* (May 1964), 37–42.

The Urban Teacher: Career and Training

Career patterns. Becker's report of interviews with Chicago public school teachers pointed out that the career line of these teachers was typically horizontal rather than vertical. That is, rather than moving up through a hierarchy of ranked positions, these teachers moved among the available positions at one level. This typically involved moving from the slum school, to which new teachers were first assigned, to better neighborhoods in the city or to the suburbs.[28] As Hodgkinson puts it, a few teachers become resigned to teaching in the slum areas (and Becker describes the modes of accommodation by which some of the Chicago teachers managed this) but "most yearn for the neat, orderly, docile children, the well-equipped classroom, and the sunlit teacher's lounge of the suburban school."[29] In remarks to the 1963 meeting of the American Association of Colleges for Teacher Education, the Dean of Chicago Teachers College North indicated that Becker's description still held good eleven years later. The effects of such career patterns upon the possibility of long-range curriculum planning and quality of instruction in the slum schools would appear to need no elaboration.

New training criteria. Conditions of this kind have led to a criticism of the teacher-education program, which is committed to preparing "the comprehensively educated teacher for the comprehensive high schools," and which succeeds only in preparing teachers who are adequate for neither the college-oriented suburbs nor for the slums.[30] Kircher believes that the decision to teach in a slum or suburban school is of the same order as the choice to teach in elementary or secondary school, and he proposes that the teacher-education program reflect the differences in preparation demanded by the different environments as well as the different levels. He suggests a five-year program for prospective suburban and slum

[28] Howard S. Becker, "The Career of the Chicago Public School Teacher," *American Journal of Sociology,* LVII (March 1952), 470–77.

[29] Harold L. Hodgkinson, *Education in Social and Cultural Perspectives* (Englewood Cliffs, N.J.: Prentice-Hall, Inc., 1962), p. 92. If reports of the experience of some teachers in wealthy suburban schools are valid, that environment also is not entirely free of psychic punishment inflicted by students who are contemptuous of teachers in their own way.

[30] Everett J. Kircher, "Teacher Education for the Slum and the Suburban School," *Proceedings of the Nineteenth Annual Meeting of the Philosophy of Education Society* (Lawrence, Kans.: The Society, 1963), pp. 214–22.

school teachers, in which the general education portion would be the same but a more academically rigorous program (and higher achievement in academic courses) would be required of those planning to teach the college-bound students of the suburbs. The program for prospective slum school teachers would need to recognize that they will employ their knowledge much as primary teachers do; that is, their knowledge would no more be taught directly to slum students than the knowledge of literature possessed by third-grade teachers is used in teaching third-grade reading. The program must also devise methods by which slum teachers would acquire a realistic acquaintance with the slum environment and with the world of work for which most slum children must be prepared. Finally, the program requires the creation of a staff of educators genuinely concerned with the task of preparing slum teachers, educators already experienced in teaching in such an environment and interested in making such teaching their area of professional study and research.

These general principles reflect the program proposed by the Dean of Teacher Education of the City University of New York,[31] based on experience with a pilot program carried on by Hunter College.[32] In the Hunter College program, students were prepared specifically for jobs in the junior high schools of slum areas in which they did their student-teaching. As student-teachers, they received not only the usual supervision from subject-matter specialists but also support from a staff member who was available for full-time consultation in the school. They also received assistance in becoming acquainted with the community served by the school through visits to such community agencies as social welfare services, police courts, religious leaders, and the editorial offices of local newspapers.

The Hunter College program seems to have demonstrated that there is sufficient idealism among young people for such a program to attract students who can become successful teachers in slum schools. Colleges and schools of education, however, should consider carefully the implications, for the teaching profession, of further differentiation in the teacher-training program. Even more

---

[31] Harry N. Rivlin, *Teachers for the Schools in Our Big Cities* (Philadelphia, Pa.: The University of Pennsylvania Press, 1962).

[32] Herbert Schueler, "Teachers for Megalopolis—The Hunter College Program," in *Strength Through Reappraisal* (Washington, D.C.: The American Association of Colleges for Teacher Education, 1963), pp. 141–49.

important, they should be concerned about the wisdom of preparing teachers for a specific environment—particularly an environment that, in its racial and social characteristics, is symptomatic of a deep illness of urban society.

CHAPTER VI

The Support and Control of the Schools

The Control of Education

The failure of the federal constitution to mention education, and the reservation to the states or to the people of "powers not delegated to the United States by the Constitution, nor prohibited by it to the States," have bestowed upon the states ultimate authority over education. Historically, schools were established by local communities. States found it necessary to assert their authority because of inequalities between the educational systems established by communities with differing resources and commitments to education. The powers and duties of the local school board are determined by the state; school board members are state officers chosen by methods determined by the state government; and the school district is an instrumentality created by the state to carry out its educational purposes.

Authority at the local level derives not only from legislative mandate and consent, but from "the general powers given to school boards to operate schools."[1] Unless unreasonable and arbitrary, the actions of school boards based upon their implied authority have been upheld by the courts. Thus school boards, the majority of which are locally elected, have been able to adapt the school program to the special needs of the local community. But the basic authority of the state remains, as illustrated by state action in both North and South to enforce or to prevent compliance with court desegregation orders; state-imposed loyalty oaths for teachers; state certification of teachers and accreditation of teacher-training institutions; and state legislation concerning instruction in specific subjects or ideas.

---

[1] American Association of School Administrators, *Schoolboard-Superintendent Relationships* (Washington, D.C.: National Education Association, 1956), p. 153.

Support of Public Education

The revenues of the public school system have come largely from the local community and the state, with a small but increasing percentage from the federal government. For the past ten years, the public schools have received approximately 56 per cent of their revenues from the local community and county. But the proportion of school revenue received from sources below the state level (largely the local community) has steadily decreased since 1929–30, when 83 per cent of school funds were so derived. The state contribution has risen steadily between 1929–30, when it was 17 per cent of total revenue, and 1949–50, when it was 40 per cent (it has remained at approximately this level ever since).

The federal government has provided financial assistance to schools in areas where federal activities have imposed special educational burdens; financed the education of veterans of World War II and the Korean War; subsidized hot lunches for school children; made available surplus property to school systems and institutions; and helped in the construction of school libraries and academic facilities in the sciences, engineering, mathematics, and modern foreign languages. The National Science Foundation has furthered research and teaching in science, and the National Defense Education Act of 1958 provided money to strengthen certain critical areas in education—particularly science, mathematics, foreign languages, and counselling.[2] In 1961, federal support of education amounted to approximately $1.5 billion in grants and payments, and $377.7 million in loans. Over $650 million went to public elementary and secondary schools, representing 4.4 per cent of their total revenues.[3] This proportion, though small, represents an increase from 0.4 per cent in 1929–30. In fact, the federal contribution has been at least 4 per cent since 1953–54.

Federal aid. The attempt to increase the federal contribution to public education has posed an important policy decision, one which affects many decisions regarding curriculum, salary schedules, and ultimately, quality of the school program. In view of the history of

[2] *It's Older Than the Constitution* (Washington, D.C.: National Education Association, Division of Federal Relations, September 1962).
[3] U.S. Department of Health, Education, and Welfare, *Progress of Public Education in the United States of America* 1962–63 (Washington, D.C.: USGPO, 1963), pp. 1, 3.

the federal contribution to education, the issue clearly relates—not to federal aid as such—but to an increase in its amount and its use for the general support of the schools instead of for specific purposes.

Opponents of increased federal aid point to the power of the federal government and its threat to freedom in education. Such an argument, according to the National Education Association, confuses fiscal responsibility with control. If the schools are to use public funds, it is only reasonable for the public to want an accounting; but this, the National Education Association argues, is not the same as federal determination of school policy, personnel, and curriculum. Pointing to the teachers of approximately one third of all public school students who now receive some portion of their salary from federal funds, the National Education Association denies that the actual record justifies fear of federal control. And in cases in which funds for aid to schools in federally impacted areas have been involved, Congress has been willing to put aside its fears on this score. For Lieberman, it is, rather, local control that interferes with freedom in education, because of the ease with which dominant groups in the community can impose their opinions upon the school. This can be seen in Southern communities, where white majorities exclude instruction critical of racial segregation, and in communities dominated by fundamentalist sects, which exclude instruction in the theory of evolution. Such interference would be more difficult, Lieberman argues, under a national system of education in which schools could continue to be the legal responsibility of states and local communities but would be controlled by national professional organizations (as is the case with medical education). The "public" character of public education, he asserts, does not rest entirely with its support and control; it refers to the quality of education as well as to its financial and organizational basis: "The qualitative referent is an education in which the search for truth is carried on regardless of what empires topple, interests collapse, or heads roll." In this sense, public education may lack a "public spirit," and the programs of privately controlled institutions may be "more free of parochial limitations than the programs in most publicly controlled institutions."[4]

Taking the problem of federal control seriously, Thayer believes

---

[4] Myron Lieberman, *The Future of Public Education* (Chicago: The University of Chicago Press, Phoenix Edition 1962), pp. 40–41.

advocates of increased federal aid face a real dilemma, particularly inasmuch as far more money than has so far been suggested in federal assistance will be needed for adequate financing of the public schools. He suggests it is unreasonable to assume that such sums would be appropriated without assurance that they will be wisely spent, or to expect wealthy states to tax themselves to improve education in poorer states without guarantees respecting the uses to which their money will be put. On the other hand, he questions the likelihood that "a centralized authority in Washington will supervise expenditures with an eye sufficiently sensitive to differences in needs among communities and in a manner best calculated to stimulate local pride and initiative and self-determination." As an alternative, he suggests regional boards, on which state departments of education, laymen, and the federal government would be represented, and which would provide for control over expenditure of federal funds and, at the same time, "the cooperative definition and realization of standards and criteria appropriate and relevant to the needs of the states and localities affected."[5]

The fears expressed by Thayer suggest one of the three major arguments for local control of education: namely, that governing is itself educative. If people have the responsibility for solving a problem, and know no one else will do it for them, they will exert themselves to understand it and note carefully the consequences of their actions, thereby enlarging their understanding and their interests. A government whose main aim is the elevation of its citizens will therefore cherish local control. It is also argued that, the closer people are to a situation, the better they will understand it and the more sensitive they will be to the special needs and circumstances involved. Conversely, the federal government is remote and consequently lacks an intimate understanding of local situations. Finally, a progressive society combines diversity in unity; it values differences and deliberately maintains those which do not imperil unity. Differences make for progress; a monolithic society is not only distasteful, it is actually self-defeating.

These principles, in the abstract, are convincing. As usual in human affairs, however, they involve a balancing of the values of

[5] V. T. Thayer, *The Role of the School in American Society* (New York: Dodd, Mead & Co., Inc., 1961), p. 513.

local control against some of its disadvantages. Lieberman points out, for example, the difficulties of making basic curriculum changes in the 21,000 high schools across the country, each of which is under local control. He also maintains that local control has obstructed educational research and the utilization of its results, so that there have been lags both in what is taught and in teaching methods. Such arguments may overestimate the localism and underestimate the possibilities of unity which exist in national associations of teachers and in facilities for the interchange of ideas and information.

More fundamental is his charge that local control is undemocratic in that it permits educational opportunity to be determined by "circumstances of race, geographical location, or economic status." The child's chances of education should not, he asserts, depend upon the fortuitous matter of where he lives and the extent to which his state government is willing to provide him with an education.[6]

Inequities under present support patterns. Present state and local patterns of support, judged by a number of indices, suggest that the quality of education received by individuals is subject to the accident of place of birth. Differences between local school districts in pupil population, area, and wealth has constituted one source of inequity. Although the reorganization of school districts reduced their number from 127,244 in 1932 to 53,000 in 1957, the report of the American Association of School Administrators Commission on School District Reorganization found the taxable wealth of the remaining districts grossly inadequate for supporting a modern twelve-grade school program, even if all districts had a sufficient number of pupils to make such a program feasible (which is not the case).[7] In states with large numbers of small districts, the richest district within a county has been found to have twenty to fifty times as much wealth per pupil as the poorest. Inadequate subject-matter preparation of teachers has been related to the demand by the smaller school for teachers who are able to teach several subjects. Conant's recommendations for improved teacher preparation, in this respect, are associated with further progress in school consolida-

---

[6] Lieberman, *op. cit.,* pp. 34–35.

[7] American Association of School Administrators, *School District Organization,* Report of the Commission on School District Reorganization (Washington, D.C.: National Education Association, 1958), p. 83.

tion. The number of school districts was reduced to 38,402 by 1961; and not only were secondary schools becoming larger, but the number of six-year high schools (which make possible a better program) was increasing.[8] The progress of school reorganization varies, however, from state to state; gross inequities still can be found—even within a single city where there are several elementary school districts.

At the state level, the average expenditures per pupil in 1961–62 ranged from $250 in Mississippi to $615 in New York (the national average was $414). Spending below $300 (and ranking forty-third to fifty-first among the fifty states and the District of Columbia) were North Carolina, West Virginia, Georgia, Arkansas, Kentucky, Alabama, South Carolina, Tennessee, and Mississippi. Those spending over $500 were New York, Alaska, New Jersey, and Illinois. Even if allowance is made for price differentials and climatic variations, the differences in the educational experience of children in the two sets of states would appear to be considerable. That these differentials affect the national interest has been argued on the basis, first, of the mobility of the American population, particularly the migration from states with inadequate economic conditions and educational facilities to more favored states. In addition, disqualification of selective service registrants for failure to pass the educational test occurs at a higher rate in some parts of the country than others, resulting in an inequitable and inefficient use of human resources.

Projected needs. It is expected that increased educational costs will aggravate existing inequities. A 19.1 per cent increase in population has been projected for the 1960–70 decade, with the largest increase among school- and college-age persons, and the smallest among those producing the income and paying the taxes that support schools and colleges. A 12.2 per cent increase is predicted in the income-producing population (ages twenty-two to sixty-four), 17.1 per cent in the five-to-thirteen age group, 42.7 per cent in the fourteen-to-seventeen age group, and 56.6 per cent in the eighteen-to-twenty-one age group.[9] Translated into educational needs, these figures mean, according to the National Education Association esti-

8 James Bryant Conant, *Education of American Teachers* (New York: McGraw-Hill Book Company, 1963), pp. 167–69, Appendix H.

9 *Population Projections, 1960–70* (Washington, D.C.: National Education Association Research Division, June 1961).

mates, an enrollment increase in elementary and secondary schools during the 1960's of approximately 8.1 million students. Although smaller than the 11 million increase in the 1950's, it probably will be more expensive, because a larger proportion of the students will be in high school, where the per pupil cost is higher. To replace teachers leaving the profession and provide the additional teachers needed to take care of increased enrollments, an average of 200,000 new teachers a year will be needed. The low birth rates of the 1930's have resulted in a shortage in the age ranges from which the majority of beginning teachers have been recruited, and competition from business and industry for college-trained personnel will make it even more difficult to recruit qualified people into teaching at present salary levels. School construction needs generally will increase along with rising enrollments.

As estimated by the National Education Association, President Eisenhower's Commission on National Goals, and the White House Conference of 1955, the cost of public schools in 1970 will be about double the 1960 figure of more than $15 billion, which itself was an increase of nearly $9.5 billion over the 1950 cost. Although some of this increase can be offset by growth in the economy, the amount needed apparently will require increasing the schools' share of total public expenditures.

To provide the additional school revenue from present sources would require increases in property taxes (the chief local source of school revenue) and in income, sales, and excise taxes (the major state sources of school revenue). In combination, state and local tax revenues have at least doubled in the decade of the 1950's. Also, there is much competition for the state dollar from other services. States have been encouraged to allocate funds to noneducational activities for which additional support, on a matching basis, has been made available by the federal government. Finally, the states must compete—first with each other (a state that raises its taxes risks a loss of industry to lower-tax states), and then with the federal government, which now collects over 80 per cent of all taxes levied in the United States (in 1890 it collected only 35 per cent). The National Education Association concludes that some states could increase their tax yields, but to find state and local funds in the quantities needed would require drastic readjustments in patterns of taxation. This would mean drastic adjustments in priorities:

either taxes must be raised, or more of the tax dollar must be expended on education—or, probably, both.

Differences in the resources of the various states are considerable. The personal income per pupil enrolled in 1959 in Delaware, for example, was $17,036; in Mississippi, $4,040. New York, to spend an average of $559 per pupil in 1959–60, spent 3.8 per cent of its personal income; South Carolina, to spend $205 per pupil, had to spend 4.3 per cent of its personal income. The National Education Association takes, as an index of the capacity of a state to support education, the income left citizens after payments for personal taxes and the basic necessities of life. Division of this residual income by the number of school-age children in the state provides the total personal income available per child for all additional expenditures of every kind, public and private. On this basis, in 1955, Massachusetts, the least wealthy of the eight richest states, had almost four times the residual buying power ($5046) per child as did West Virginia, the richest of the poor states ($1456). The eight richest states had, on the average, more than five times as many disposable dollars as the eight poorest states.[10]

Given these inequalities, but wishing to preserve as decentralized a school system as possible, the Committee on Economic Development has proposed restricting federal aid to states with extremely low personal incomes relative to the number of schoolchildren. The Committee suggests 80 per cent of the national average, based on current expenditures per pupil in average daily attendance, as a standard for school expenditures. In 1957–58, eleven states fell below—in some cases, far below—this 80 per cent minimum. A formula that would take into account the level of existing effort to support schools locally (lest the incentive to increase local support be eliminated) and the amount by which the states' personal income per student in ADA (Average Daily Attendance) falls short of 80 per cent of the national average, would, the Committee contends, enable the federal government to equalize educational opportunity in the states needing help for a moderate annual expenditure.[11]

---

[10] Educational Policies Commission, *National Policy and the Financing of the Public Schools* (Washington, D.C.: National Education Association, 1959), pp. 15–18.

[11] Committee for Economic Development, *Paying for Better Schools* (New York: The Committee, 1959).

Public Support of Private Schools

The problem of "double taxation." One of the important obstacles to recent legislative attempts to provide increased federal aid to education has been the controversy over the exclusion of private—and, more specifically, parochial—schools from such aid, as they are now generally excluded by the provisions of state constitutions and federal legislation. Leaders of the Roman Catholic school system, which constitutes the bulk of the independent schools, have claimed that sectarian as well as public schools should receive public funds, and they have been successful in rallying support for their opposition to legislation that does not honor that right. Inclusion of sectarian schools in the federal aid program, as the Church sees it, is justified clearly on the basis of the principle of distributive justice:

> . . . a government which collects school taxes from all citizens is obligated by distributive justice to appropriate an equitable share to all qualified schools rendering a public service. . . . [I]t follows that federal and state laws forbidding tax aid to Catholic and other qualified nonpublic schools are unjust and ought to be repealed and amended.[12]

Catholic schools, it is argued, render a public service in preparing young people for their civic responsibilities; and they provide such preparation for a sizable proportion of the children of the nation (in 1960, about one out of every six children), thereby relieving the community of that financial burden. Furthermore, in the United States it is not merely parents' privilege but their right to send their children to sectarian schools. Such a right, however, is already penalized by the "double taxation" to which such parents are subject. Parental freedom of choice would be meaningless were the existence of sectarian schools threatened or seriously curtailed by restricting governmental aid to public schools. Such a policy, it is argued further, militates against the diversity needed and esteemed by this society. In the current educational crisis, every valid educational resource available should be used. Catholic schools conform to the standards set for public schools in matters of accreditation, teacher certification, and codes regulating buildings, health, and safety. Fi-

[12] Msgr. William E. McManus, "The Administration and Financing of Catholic Schools," *Phi Delta Kappan*, XLV (December 1963), 132–35.

nally, restriction of federal aid to public schools would limit the free exercise of religion, for thereby the federal government would be put in the position of "telling parents that they will receive no assistance for the education of their children if they insist upon sending them to schools where religious and secular knowledge are integrated."[13]

Constitutional considerations.   Opposition to the use of federal funds to provide general support to sectarian schools has been based ultimately upon interpretation of the First Amendment to the Constitution: "Congress shall make no law respecting an establishing of religion, or prohibiting the free exercise thereof." Although education was the responsibility of the states, which were not under the restrictions of the First Amendment, most of the states have forbidden the use of public funds for the support of schools established to teach sectarian doctrines. It was not until the Fourteenth Amendment—or, more specifically, the Supreme Court's interpretation of that Amendment—that the guarantees of the First Amendment were held to apply to the states. Application of the religious clause of the First Amendment to the states was stated explicitly by the Court in *Everson* v. *Board of Education* (330 U.S. 1, 1947):

> Neither a state nor the federal government can set up a church. Neither can pass laws which aid one religion, aid all religions, or prefer one religion over another. Neither can force or influence a person to go to or to remain away from church against his will or force him to profess a belief or disbelief in any religion. No person can be punished for entertaining or professing religious beliefs or disbeliefs, for church attendance or nonattendance. No tax in any amount, large or small, can be levied to support any religious activities or institutions, whatever they may be called nor whatever form they may adopt to teach or practice religion. Neither a state nor the federal government can, openly or secretly, participate in the affairs of any religious organizations or groups and vice versa. In the words of Jefferson, the clause against establishment of religion by law was intended to erect "a wall of separation between church and state."

That this decision did not settle the matter, however, is indicated by the fact that this was the New Jersey case in which, by a five-to-four decision, the Court found the use of public funds to pay for the

---

13 "The Study by the Legal Department of the National Catholic Welfare Conference on the Constitutionality of the Inclusion of Church-Related Schools in Federal Aid to Education," *National Education Association Journal* (May 1962), p. 27.

transportation of children to parochial schools a constitutional exercise of state power. Furthermore, this case had been preceded by a decision (*Cochran* v. *Louisiana State Board of Education* [281 U.S. 370, 1930]) in which the Court found the State of Louisiana had not violated constitutional protections in supplying free textbooks to children in parochial as well as public schools. In the latter case, the decision was based on the principle that the aid had benefited only the child and the state itself, not the sectarian school. In the Everson case, however, it was admitted that state aid in transporting children to parochial schools helped these schools, but this aid, the Court held, was not direct, but incidental to the provision of governmental services to which all people are entitled, whatever their religion. The Court compared state provisions intended to guarantee free transportation to parochial school students with state-paid policemen detailed to protect such children from traffic hazards, and with "fire protection, connections for sewage disposal, public highways and sidewalks" provided by public funds—services which, if cut off from church schools, would also make it more difficult for them to operate:

> We must be careful in protecting the citizens of New Jersey against state-established churches, to be sure that we do not inadvertently prohibit New Jersey from extending its general state law benefits to all its citizens without regard to their religious belief.

The Everson decision, then, unlike the Cochran decision, admitted the constitutionality of state aid to religious schools when that aid is incidental to the provision of benefits to which all citizens are otherwise entitled. On this point do Roman Catholic spokesmen base their claim that private nonprofit schools may *constitutionally* be included as beneficiaries of federal aid to education.[14] The decision raised the knotty problem of how to distinguish between incidental aid and direct aid. The difficulties of such a distinction are illustrated by the fact that state courts have disagreed on the constitutionality of transportation laws such as those passed in New Jersey: in some states such legislation has been held constitutional, as benefiting the child rather than the schools; in others it has been held in violation of the First Amendment. There are other problems of classification: the provision of hot lunches to school children, health care for all children, and what have been called quasi-instructional services—

---

[14] *Ibid.*, p. 28.

record-keeping, diagnostic services, and placement and follow-up of high school graduates, for example.[15]

The difficulties of drawing the line between direct support and incidental benefits have led the U.S. Department of Health, Education, and Welfare to conclude that "it is easier to determine what the First Amendment forbids than what it allows." Unconstitutional proposals that can be "readily identified," according to the Department's lawyers, include across-the-board grants and loans to church schools and tuition payments for all parochial school pupils. On the child-benefit theory, bus transportation and collateral benefits such as milk and lunches are permitted. Permissible also are loans "for special purposes not closely related to religious instruction." Under the National Defense Education Act, for example, church schools may borrow funds for equipment used in teaching science, mathematics, and foreign languages. In this case, specific national purposes are promoted, their relationship to the religious function of a church school is remote, and the requirement that the loans be repaid makes it unlikely that the church school will be able to free its own funds for religious purposes. The difficulty of separating secular and sectarian education in church school curricula makes it difficult, however, to envisage other directions in which the principle of special-purpose loans could be extended.[16]

The sense that its cause is just, reinforced by the rising costs of construction and personnel for a separate school system, promises continued opposition by the Church to federal legislation that excludes parochial schools from its benefits. In light of this, two alternative policies have emerged. One is the shared-time program, by which parochial school students would attend public schools for part of a day or week to receive instruction in such fields as science, mathematics, or vocational education. This would transfer part of the burden of personnel, equipment, and construction from parochial schools to public schools, which would need additional funds. Such funds would come to the public school district, hopefully avoiding the church-state controversy, although open to attack as disguised state aid to religious schools. With respect to the nature of

---

15 James M. Hughes, *Education in America* (New York: Harper & Row, Publishers, 1960), pp. 327–30.

16 "Memorandum by the Legal Department of HEW on the Impact of the First Amendment to the Constitution Upon Federal Aid to Education," *National Education Journal* (May 1962), 26–27.

federal aid itself, there is a tendency to push for expansion of categorical aid—aid for specific purposes—to an extent that would approximate general aid. This is the position recently taken by the Educational Policies Commission of the National Education Association, which, in *Educational Responsibilities of the Federal Government,* has urged larger appropriations for categorical aid and more categories of aid, and at lower levels, particularly for the elementary school. In 1965 the Johnson Administration proposed a $1.3 billion federal school aid bill that appears to embody a number of the principles discussed: categorical rather than general aid; an "impacted areas" approach through focus upon aid to children of low-income families; and use of the principles of child benefits and indirect aid as the basis of contributing to the education of children in nonpublic and parochial schools.

Religion in the Public Schools

The maintenance of the separation of church and state has also raised the perplexing issue of religious instruction in the public schools themselves. The creators of the common school faced this problem immediately, Horace Mann noting in his Twelfth Annual Report that "our noble system of Free Schools for the whole people" was being denounced as "irreligious and anti-Christian." In reply, Mann outlined the arguments against any sectarian instruction in a school attended by all the children of the community and supported by the taxes of all. He also announced that the Bible was in the schools of Massachusetts, and "if any man's creed is to be found in the Bible, and the Bible is in the schools, then that man's creed is in the schools." Mann's belief in the nonsectarian character of the Bible may have been naïve, but many continue to make the same assumption, for which the homogeneity of Mann's society provided far more excuse than does contemporary America.

Released time. The sixty years that followed Mann's last Report witnessed progress in the creation of a genuinely nonsectarian school, although it varied with the ethnic composition and religious sensitivities of the community. Thayer identifies 1913 as the year in which this trend was reversed. By 1946, thirteen states had made the reading of the Bible compulsory in all public schools and in twenty-four states it was specifically permitted. In 1948, when the

U.S. Supreme Court handed down the McCollum decision (*McCollum* v. *Board of Education* [333 U.S. 203, 1948]), approximately 2500 communities were providing religious instruction through the public schools on a released-time basis for nearly 2 million pupils.[17] A survey of state supreme court decisions on Bible reading, from 1890 to 1952, led Bolmeier to conclude that there was a "preponderance of jurisdiction validating Bible reading in the public schools," in particular when the teacher was forbidden to comment on passages read and pupils who disapproved were not required to participate in the exercises.[18]

In 1948, the Supreme Court ruled against a system of released time that allowed religious instruction on school premises, as was the case in the Champaign, Illinois, school system (*McCollum* v. *Board of Education*). A dismissed-time program of religious instruction, however, in which students were released during school hours to go to their various religious centers for instruction while other children stayed in school and continued their secular studies, was declared constitutional (*Zorach* v. *Clauson* [343 U.S. 306, 1951]). In this decision, the Court described the government as "neutral" in the competition between sects, but noted that there was "no constitutional requirement which makes it necessary for government to be hostile to religion and to throw its weight against efforts to widen the effective scope of religious influence." As a consequence, the government—and its agent, the school—"can close its doors or suspend its operations as to those who want to repair to their religious sanctuary for worship or instruction."

Bible reading and prayer. In the 1960's, the Supreme Court has found Bible reading and prayer in the public schools unconstitutional. *Engel* v. *Vitale* (370 U.S. 421, 1962) involved a "nonsectarian" prayer composed by the New York State Board of Regents to be said daily in the New York classrooms. Justice Black wrote for the majority:

> Neither the fact that the prayer may be denominationally neutral nor the fact that its observance on the part of the students is voluntary can serve to free it from the limitations of the establishment clause, as it might from the free-exercise clause, of the First Amend-

---

17 Thayer, *op. cit.*, pp. 374–75, fn. 36, 406–407.

18 E. C. Bolmeier, "Legality and Propriety of Religious Instruction in the Public Schools," *Educational Forum*, XX (May 1956), 473–82. By permission of Kappa Delta Pi, an Honor Society in Education.

ment, both of which are operative against the states by virtue of the Fourteenth Amendment.

But *Engel* v. *Vitale* did not deal with Bible reading, or with recitation of the Lord's Prayer; these were issues raised by *Abington School District* v. *Schempp* (371 U.S. 807, 1963). In declaring such practices unconstitutional, the majority decision of the Court fell back, as in *Zorach* v. *Clauson,* on the "rule of neutrality." Agreeing that the state may not oppose or show hostility to religion, thereby "preferring those who believe in no religion over those who do believe," Justice Clark denied that the decision had any such effect, and added:

> ... it might well be said that one's education is not complete without a study of comparative religion or the history of religion and its relationship to the advancement of civilization. It certainly may be said that the Bible is worthy of study for its literary and historic qualities. Nothing we have said here indicates that such study of the Bible or of religion, when presented objectively as part of a secular program of education, may not be effected consistent with the First Amendment. But the exercises here do not fall into those categories. They are religious exercises, required by the states in violation of the command of the First Amendment that the government maintain strict neutrality, neither aiding nor opposing religion.

"Factual" instruction. The "factual" study of religion, as an essential part of general education and the best means of filling the "vacuum caused by the avoidance of religion," had already been recommended by the American Council on Education and the Educational Policies Commission of the National Education Association.[19] The latter advocated that schools should seek deliberately to insure that "the moral and spiritual values which are shared by the members of all religious faiths" are exemplified by "the spirit of the school and its teachers," and that they permeate guidance functions, special activities, hobbies and clubs, sports, and the teaching of organized subject matter.

Even if public school teachers are, or can be, fitted to present religion "factually," will their professional status, and the local

---

[19] American Council on Education, *The Function of the Public Schools in Dealing with Religion, A Report on the Exploratory Study Made by the Committee on Religion and Education* (Washington, D.C.: National Education Association, 1953); and Educational Policies Commission, *Moral and Spiritual Values in the Public Schools* (Washington, D.C.: Educational Policies Commission, 1951).

milieu in which they work, enable them to do so? The danger of mistaking agreement on moral abstractions for consensus on a concrete and meaningful level—in local communities, among teachers, and in teacher-training institutions—casts doubt on the Commission's report. On the other hand, those who are now attempting to overturn the Court's decisions need to take seriously the Commission's reminder that moral education is the joint responsibility of all social institutions—home, church, government, and the mass media, as well as the schools:

> The personnel of the public schools may become more than a little weary of being expected to carry practically the whole load of education in moral and spiritual areas, whilst they are taunted as "Godless" and ineffective if they do not succeed in overcoming the powerful maleducative forces which are permitted to flourish in almost every community.[20]

---

[20] *Ibid.*, p. 84.

CHAPTER VII

Status and Roles of the Teacher

The effect of social forces upon the teaching occupation, Charters points out, is both selective and formative; that is, such forces help to determine who enters the profession and directly affect those within it.[1] The prestige of an occupation also helps to determine the number and quality of those who enter it. Beginning with the work of Counts, surveys of the prestige of the teaching profession have shown that, in the public mind, the college professor is superior to the public school teacher, the high school teacher outranks the elementary school teacher, and teaching is in the "second or third tier among the professions."[2] In Counts' list of forty-five occupations, the average rank of college professors was second; superintendents of schools, seventh; high school teachers, tenth; elementary school teachers, thirteenth; and rural school teachers, nineteenth.[3] In 1947, the National Opinion Research Center asked a cross section of the American people to rank ninety occupations on a five-point scale. College professors ranked seventh (preceded by U.S. Supreme Court Justices, physicians, state governors, Cabinet members in the federal government, diplomats in the U.S. foreign service, and mayors of large cities) and the public school teacher ranked thirty-sixth.[4] A year later, 1676 Indiana University students—mostly first-semester freshmen—given a list of only eighteen occupations, ranked college professors third (following physician and lawyer), high school teachers fifth, and elementary school teachers sixth.[5]

---

[1] W. W. Charters, Jr., "The Social Background of Teaching," in *Handbook of Research on Teaching*, edited by N. L. Gage (Chicago: Rand McNally & Co., 1963), p. 717.

[2] David C. Beardslee and Donald D. O'Dowd, "Students and the Occupational World," in *The American College*, edited by Nevitt Sanford (New York: John Wiley & Sons, Inc., 1962), p. 616; see Table 1, p. 609.

[3] George S. Counts, "The Social Status of Occupations," *School Review*, XXXIII (January 1925), 16–27; see Table 1, pp. 20–21.

[4] "Jobs and Occupations: A Popular Evaluation," in *Class, Status, and Power*, edited by Richard Bendix and Seymour Lipset (New York: The Free Press of Glencoe, Inc., 1953), pp. 411–26.

[5] R. W. Richey, W. H. Fox, and C. E. Fausset, "Prestige Ranks of Teaching," *Occupations*, XXX (October 1951), 33–35.

These results coincided with those of a 1934 study, except in the case of elementary school teachers, who then ranked seventh. In the late 1950's, random samples of freshmen and seniors at four colleges in New England (a small, highly selective men's liberal arts college, a highly selective private women's college, and a college of arts and sciences at a state university) were asked their views about fifteen "high-level" occupations. The male students were asked to "rate each of the occupational positions according to how much *you* would like to enter them if you were free to make the choice without regard for training, ability, or time and expense required for specialized study." School teachers were sixth in a list led by college professors, lawyers, doctors, business executives, and scientists.[6]

Determinants of Status

Social-class origins and salary. The status of any occupation is determined by a number of interrelated factors, including the social origins, income, power, and amount of formal education of its members.

Public school teachers are recruited largely from the lower-middle class and, to some extent of late, from the upper-lower class —a tendency that will not add prestige to the occupation, whatever its desirability on other grounds. Any consideration of the effect of income on the status of the school teacher needs to take into account the distinction between beginning, average, and maximum salaries. The median scheduled salaries for beginning classroom teachers with bachelor's degrees in school systems of 400,000 or more in 1962–63 was $4800. The estimated annual starting salaries paid men with bachelor's degrees that year were $5616 in sales, $5856 in accounting, and $6648 in engineering.[7] Although the National Education Association believes that $6000 is needed to place teaching in an "excellent" position to compete with the beginning salaries of other college-trained professional personnel, the starting salary for teachers is more competitive than maximum salaries. The latter are generally only a few thousand dollars higher, a situation unattractive to able people, as even Koerner, denying the

6 Donald D. O'Dowd and David C. Beardslee, "The Student Image of the School Teacher," *Phi Delta Kappan,* XLII (March 1961), 250–54.

7 *National Education Association Research Bulletin,* XLI, 2 (May 1963), 48, Table 4.

"myth of low teacher salaries," admits. Fewer than 10 per cent of all teachers in the United States earned salaries of $7500 or more in 1961–62. The average salary of public school teachers appears to be more comparable to that of industrial workers than to that of professional groups. According to the U.S. Commissioner of Education, the average salary of classroom teachers in large urban centers in 1960–61 was $6096, compared with $9474 for persons in eight other professions requiring a college degree. The Commissioner also pointed out that nearly 40 per cent of male teachers held a second job; and studies have shown that the "moonlighting" done by teachers often is in low-status positions.

The income status of teachers is affected by the predominance of women in the profession; they constitute about 70 per cent of all employed teachers and their pay often represents a second income. For most women, teaching is what has been described as a "contingent" rather than a "dominant" role.[8] which has important implications for both average salaries and the professionalization of teaching.[9] Another index of status is the average annual leaving rate which, for the nation as a whole, is estimated to be 10–15 per cent of the total teaching population.[10]

Educational preparation. Salary levels are related, in part, to the amount of formal education, itself a determinant of prestige. T. M. Stinnett, Assistant Executive Secretary for Professional Development and Welfare of the National Education Association, remarks on the slowness with which teaching has shifted from the learning-on-the-job concept to college and university preservice preparation. Stinnett's concept of extended professional preparation for the teacher consists of a bachelor's degree for the beginning teacher and, for the "fully qualified" teacher, at least an additional year of study after the initial teaching experience. This may be compared with the seven years required for medicine and theology and the six years required for such professions as dentistry, osteopathy, veterinary medicine, and law. Even the lower standards for teachers

[8] Ward S. Mason, R. J. Dressel, and R. K. Bain, "Sex Role and the Career Orientations of Beginning Teachers," *Harvard Educational Review,* XXIX (Fall 1959), 370–83.

[9] Myron Lieberman, *Education as a Profession* (Englewood Cliffs, N.J.: Prentice-Hall, Inc., 1956), pp. 241–55.

[10] Willavene Wolf and William Wolf, "Teacher Dropouts—A Professional Lament," in *Teaching in America,* edited by Anthony C. Riccio and Frederick R. Cyphert (New York: Charles E. Merrill Books Inc., 1962).

are not completely met. In 1961, only forty-four states required four college years of preparation for beginning teachers in the elementary schools; in 1960 only 75 per cent of the employed elementary teachers had graduated from four-year teacher-education programs or had completed preparation beyond the bachelor's degree. In 1961, only one state (Arkansas) would certify beginning high school teachers below the bachelor's degree level; Arizona, California, and the District of Columbia required five years of college preparation. Individuals with substandard qualifications, however, are allowed to teach. Kinney estimates that, in the country as a whole, about one teacher in thirteen is teaching with substandard preparation. "The overriding rule of certification standards," he asserts, "is the law of supply and demand," in contrast with licensing practices in other professions, in which standards for admission are unaffected by personnel shortages: "In law, or medicine, for example, the unqualified practitioner not only goes unlicensed—he goes to jail."[11] Four eminent educators have commented that

> Compared to other professions, standards for certification for teachers and specialized educational practice are low. Although comparisons are often made between teaching and such professions as medicine and law, in reality standards for certification compare more realistically with those for nursing, medical technician service, and social work.[12]

Power and influence. Status has also been associated with power, or the ability to control the behavior of others. Lieberman suggests that this explains the differences in prestige among various groups within education—the college professor, the high school teacher, and the elementary teacher—for "control of adult behavior is more significant from the standpoint of occupational status than control of adolescent or child behavior."[13] In amount of power that teachers hold, however, few could outrank the business executive or labor leader. A commitment to the principle of security rather than material reward, a lack of knowledgeability and consid-

---

[11] Lucien B. Kinney, *Certification in Education* (Englewood Cliffs, N.J.: Prentice-Hall, Inc., 1964), p. 119.

[12] Lindley J. Stiles, A. S. Barr, Harl R. Douglass, and Hubert H. Mills, *Teacher Education in the United States* (New York: The Ronald Press Company, 1960), p. 302. Copyright © 1960 The Ronald Press Company.

[13] Myron Lieberman, *Education as a Profession* (Englewood Cliffs, N.J.: Prentice-Hall, Inc., 1956), p. 471.

erable timidity about political action, and a sense of isolation from
the life of the society were the chief characteristics of teachers of a
school system in what Terrien called Port City. He concluded that
the status of these teachers could best be described as "unresolved":

> The status of teachers is somewhere on a continuum. At one end
> they are the cultural surrogates, and as such, have "power" in the
> primitive sense of the word. They operate in the realm of thought,
> where they cannot be controlled—hence they are to be suspected
> and feared. At the other end of the continuum they are the house-
> wives of the culture—the ones concerned with maintenance and
> continuity, and hence the conservators. They have the role often
> assigned in primitive societies to old men, the aged, and the infirm—
> that of trainers of children. But most of all, they are the sanctioning
> agents for the young, the guardians of morals, the arbiters of con-
> duct, and it is in this status that they are remembered by all adults
> from their own childhood. In truth, teachers constitute a kind of
> conscience in society, and their status is that of the conscience—
> recognized as fundamentally important, but neglected as much as
> possible.[14]

Stereotypes

As Grambs points out, all kinds of jobs are called teaching, from
drama and football coaching to educational testing and counseling,
although few common qualities are shared by the head football
coach and the head of the English department.[15] In the case of teaching, however, as with other occupations, people operate with stereo-
types that undoubtedly affect the results of prestige ratings.

Over thirty years ago McGill studied the teacher stereotype by
presenting a group of photographs to students for identification by
occupation. Only three of the pictures were of teachers, and two of
the three were identified as teachers more frequently than could be
accounted for by chance. Reasons the students gave for the identification stressed facial expressions that indicated an unflattering
image of the teaching profession.[16] The current stereotype, according to Chilcott's evidence from one community, is rather "formless"

---

[14] Frederic Terrien, "The Occupational Roles of Teachers," *Journal of Educational Sociology*, XXIX (September 1955), 14–20.

[15] Jean D. Grambs, "The Roles of the Teacher," in *The Teacher's Role in American Society*, edited by Lindley J. Stiles, Fourteenth Yearbook of the John Dewey
Society (New York: Harper & Row, Publishers, 1957), Chap. 6.

[16] Kenneth McGill, "The School Teacher Stereotype," *Journal of Educational
Sociology*, IV (1931), 642–50.

—which he interprets to mean that the traditional stereotype of the "stern, dignified, reserved" person has broken down, but is yet to be replaced with a new construct. He believes that the new stereotype, however, will consist of "a married woman, attractive and youthful in appearance, who commands considerable community respect."[17]

The O'Dowd and Beardslee study is also optimistic in showing that college students today hold a more positive conception of the school teacher than do the laymen and college faculty members. College undergraduates were found to have a high regard for teaching as a role for men. These investigators concluded that teaching as a career would be selected by a much higher percentage of male college graduates if it were not for the financial and social-status limitations associated with it.[18] The college students whom they questioned conceived of school teachers as lacking in strength, activity, hardness, assertiveness, and confidence; which corresponds interestingly with the results of a study of personality characteristics of "veteran" teachers.[19] Although the teacher, as seen by these students, is "realistic about life and adaptable in habits," and "fully in touch with real problems," his role "does not call for or permit the expression of strong, vigorous sentiments." The positive aspects of the school teacher included unselfish devotion to people, sensitivity and wisdom, and concern for artistic and cultural matters. The teacher was contrasted with the college professor as "more unselfishly devoted to people" and as "more normal, clean-cut, conservative . . . than the individualistic, radical, colorful, and interesting professor." The college faculty members who replied to the same questionnaire exhibited the same pattern of beliefs about school teachers, but gave significantly lower ratings on a variety of desirable traits. There was no evidence, however, that this commonly known attitude of college professors toward public school teachers had affected the opinions of their students.[20]

---

17 John H. Chilcott, "The School Teacher Stereotype: A New Look," *Journal of Educational Sociology,* XXXIV (May 1960), 389–90.

18 O'Dowd and Beardslee, *op. cit.,* p. 250.

19 Egon G. Guba, P. W. Jackson, and C. E. Bidwell, "Occupational Choice and the Teaching Career," *Educational Research Bulletin,* XXXVIII (January 1959), 1–13.

20 O'Dowd and Beardslee, *op. cit.,* p. 253.

Roles of the Teacher

By definition, the roles of the teacher consist of expectations for his behavior, and it would appear that the source of these expectations would provide a convenient basis for classification of the role. The two major sources would be the community, on the one hand, and, on the other, the school organization—including the expectations of adults (superiors and colleagues) and students (particularly in the classroom). The community, however, also has some expectations concerning the teacher's classroom role (as disciplinarian, for example), administrators have some expectations concerning the teacher's community role, and provision should be made for the teacher's own definition of his role as influenced by professional groups, including teacher-training institutions. In any case, Grambs' warning that role definitions are affected by variations in circumstances should be noted. The change from a rural to an urban society is particularly important in view of the fact that much of the study of teacher roles has involved rural teachers. Different social classes may have different expectations of the teacher, and differences in values, from traditional to emergent, clearly would affect role expectations. Community history and tradition will vary, and there may be unique circumstances that result in a stress on some role behaviors and indifference to others.

Teachers as models for the young. *Model* here is usually taken in the moral sense, describing the "special code of behavior" by which teachers are expected to live. The moral code relates to smoking, drinking, marriage, dating, card-playing, church attendance, dress, dancing, and the like. The rural-urban shift undoubtedly has brought about some relaxation in such codes of behavior: the city provides anonymity, and the standards of an urban society are less rigid than those of the rural population studied by Greenhoe.[21] Change has been clearly documented in the case of marriage. In 1923, 77 per cent of the city school systems replying to a National Education Association survey did not appoint married women as teachers, compared with 58 per cent in 1941 and 8 per cent in 1951.

---

[21] Florence Greenhoe, *Community Contacts and Participation of Teachers* (Washington, D.C.: American Council on Public Affairs, 1941), p. 51; see also Hulda Grobman and Vynce A. Hines, "Teacher as a Citizen," in *The Teacher's Role in American Society, op. cit.,* pp. 140–41.

In 1941, the employed teacher who married could continue in service on the same basis as the unmarried teacher in only 30 per cent of the school systems; ten years later, marriage had no effect on the woman teacher's career in 90 per cent of the reporting cities.[22] A recent National Education Association survey revealed only a tiny minority of teachers admitting to feeling restrictions on their personal lives (rural teachers reported somewhat more restriction than urban teachers).[23] These responses, it should be noted, represent how teachers *perceived* the amount of restriction on their personal life, which depends upon the extent to which they already have internalized community expectations. There is some reason to believe that teachers do accept the code and condemn colleagues who do not live up to it.[24] In any event, a sizable minority of teachers still work in rural districts and, because of the teacher's association with the young, it may be assumed that stricter demands on behavior will always be made upon teachers than upon the population in general.

The "model" role of the teacher has been considered by Brookover in the wider context of the socialization function of the school in an urbanized, segmented society.[25] He criticizes the school for providing youth with a range of models that is generally limited to the local community and "proper" middle-class behavior, whereas widespread mobility, particularly from rural to urban areas, demands an understanding of behavior in many parts of society. Students rarely see leaders of lower-status groups, such as labor leaders, who, Brookover suggests, are more realistic models for lower-status pupils than are managerial or professional people. He points also to the small proportion of men in teaching, and the consequent lack of male models for boys.[26] In secondary schools men represent nearly as large a proportion of the teaching staff as women, but the effeminate stereotype of the male teacher may reduce his effectiveness,

---

22 C. N. Morris, "Career Patterns of Teachers," in *The Teacher's Role in American Society, op. cit.,* p. 254.

23 "The Status of the American Public School Teacher," *National Educational Association Research Bulletin,* XXXV, 1 (February 1957).

24 Wilbur B. Brookover, *A Sociology of Education* (New York: American Book Company, 1955), p. 259.

25 *Ibid.,* Chap. 13.

26 See also Martin B. Loeb, "Social Role and Sexual Identity in Adolescent Males: A Study of Culturally Provided Deprivation," in *Education and Culture,* edited by George D. Spindler (New York: Holt, Rinehart & Winston, Inc., 1963), Chap. 15.

and also partly account for the importance placed on athletics and the coaching role in high schools. Elsewhere, Brookover points out that evidence is lacking on the extent to which teachers actually do serve as models, whatever the community might expect. He suggests that the effectiveness of teachers in this respect may depend upon the extent to which they reinforce behavior common to the youth's family, and that in some cases students may be unable to identify with the teacher to any significant extent. He proposes an investigation of the effect of models provided by teachers of different social classes—the upper-class teacher (not often found in the public schools), the middle-class teacher (both established and striving), and teachers unranked in the stratification system.[27]

As idealist, person of culture, and pioneer in ideas. As "idealist," the teacher is expected to be "impractical," "theoretical," and less interested in material success than are others in society. Not only the public, but most teachers, regard union membership as inappropriate; the use of the strike is condemned not only by the public but by the majority of teachers as well. This attitude is also related to the "professional" role of teachers, and the National Education Association's advocacy of "sanctions" instead of strikes to ameliorate the economic situation of teachers is justified in professional-role terms.

Closely related to the idealistic role is the expectation that the teacher will be interested in art, music, and literature. Here the community is ambivalent: such interests make many people uneasy, and contribute to the "stranger" role of the teacher, but at the same time parents want the "finer things of life" for their children. Teachers may indeed become models for children who wish to escape the Philistinism of the community or their parents. According to Grambs, however, this role may be part of community mythology; although it may have been true years ago: ". . . now the teacher is rarely a real intellectual. He may be as scornful of cultural activities as his neighbors. His knowledge of the world of ideas is often narrow." Hopefully this, if true, is a backhanded way of testifying to the elevation of educational attainment in the general population, and indicating that the public school teacher has lost cultural prominence because he is no longer, as in the early rural environment,

---

[27] Wilbur B. Brookover, "Teachers and the Stratification of American Society," *Harvard Educational Review,* XXIII (Fall 1953), 257–67.

one of the few in the community who has read books and is interested in ideas. Changes in the social origin of teachers may be relevant to changes in their role, as may the proliferation of teacher types resulting from proliferation of subject-matter fields; athletic coaches and teachers of business subjects or home economics scarcely resemble the old-time classical scholar.

Closely related also is the role of the teacher as pioneer in the world of ideas—and, hence, as a radical (this, again, despite evidence to the contrary). However nonintellectual the teacher's interest may be, he inevitably must be dealing with ideas, and thus tends to arouse the suspicion of the community. The public, recognizing thought to be potentially dangerous, has attempted to control teachers by means of loyalty oaths and other devices.

As sociological stranger. The teacher's role as a "stranger" in the community in which he teaches is based, in part, upon studies of teachers' participation in community life and, in part, upon the career pattern of movement from school to school in different communities. A recent study found that only one third of today's teachers are living in the city in which they lived as children, although the teacher in the big city was more likely to be a "home-grown" product than the small-town teacher.[28] When asked how they felt about their relationship to the life of the community in which they taught, 90 per cent of rural teachers and 86 per cent of urban teachers indicated that they felt "accepted"; less than 1 per cent of either group felt "ignored" or "rejected."[29]

Greenhoe's study, conducted over twenty years ago, found teachers' participation in the community to be predominantly through membership in religious and professional groups, rather than through civic, political, or economic-interest groups. The National Education Association study in 1957 showed a similar pattern, including definite opposition by teachers to activity in partisan politics. This attitude has been defended on the grounds that the teacher should remain neutral on controversial issues, in order to preserve the objectivity necessary to good teaching. Greenhoe, however, argued that community participation would improve teaching by familiarizing teachers with the problems of community concerns

---

[28] "Teachers in Public Schools," *National Education Association Research Bulletin,* XLI, 1, (February 1963), 26.
[29] "Status of the American Public School Teacher," *op. cit.,* p. 32.

and acquainting them with the environment of their pupils. When Brookover attempted to test this hypothesis, he found no significant relationships between community participation and teaching effectiveness as measured by gains of information made by pupils.[30] His criterion of gains in knowledge of American history may have been too indirectly related to participation in the life of a specific community. In any event, teachers may define their own roles on the assumption that objectivity precludes too close an identification with community life.

According to Grobman and Hines, even the voting and registration habits of teachers are not equal to those of other college graduates or those with comparable professional standing, although teachers do surpass the general public. Teachers "have not been conspicuously in the fore on leading intelligent discussions of political affairs or of speaking out in support of the rights of others," and have even been conspicuous by their relative absence from such nonpartisan groups as the League of Women Voters.[31] Full participation in civic and social groups, however, requires "educational qualifications, adequate income, control over blocks of time, and social prestige or status," and of these "the teacher may have only the college degree."[32]

As professional. In the sense that the community views the teacher as an expert both in subject matter and in the skill of communicating it, the "professional" role of the teacher is a community expectation. Certainly, as educational requirements for certification are raised, this is increasingly the teacher's own definition of his role. The "ideal" teacher-education program envisioned by educators provides one source of specifications for the professional role. This program is characterized by a proper balance of professional education, subject-matter specialization, and liberal education. The professional part of the program includes not only a grasp of methods and some practice in the teaching of a given subject matter, but also a knowledge of the theoretical foundations for these methods in the psychology of learning, child development, and the social, historical, and philosophical foundations of education. Within in-

---

[30] Wilbur B. Brookover, "The Relation of Social Factors to Teaching Ability," *Journal of Experimental Education*, LXXXIII (1945), 203–204.

[31] Grobman and Hines, *op. cit.*, pp. 122–23.

[32] Grobman and Hines, "The Private Life of the Teacher," *The Teacher's Role in American Society, op. cit.*, p. 140.

creased certification requirements, the additional hours will be devoted to increased subject-matter requirements and general education. In addition to improved mastery of subject matter, the teacher is to have a broad liberal education that will enable him at least to hold his own in a community characterized by increased educational attainment. Finally, emphasis is placed upon the ideal of continued professional growth through self-study, in-service programs organized and supported by the school system in which teaching is done, and formal study at the graduate level. According to Grambs:

> The teacher is given in his professional training an ideal of the teacher: one who is permissive, helpful, psychologically oriented in interpreting motivations, and is part of a self-respecting, socially important professional group.

Roles and Role Conflict

The potential for conflict presented by the roles described is obvious. Getzels and Guba have identified three conflicts in particular: teachers are expected to maintain a living standard and cultural tastes for which their salaries are not adequate; restrictions on community participation, and direction of that participation into particular channels, raise conflicts for individual teachers; and public willingness to dictate classroom content and procedures may conflict with the teacher's sense of professional competence.[33] Others have argued that the existence of contradictory expectations should not be overemphasized, both because the same kinds of conflicts exist in other professions, and also because they may not result in personal conflict, as the teacher fills a variety of roles at different times and in different contexts.[34]

---

[33] Jacob W. Getzels and Egon G. Guba, "The Structure of Roles and Role Conflict in the Teaching Situation," *Journal of Educational Sociology*, XXIX (1955), 330–40.

[34] Robert J. Havighurst and Bernice Neugarten, *Society and Education* (Boston: Allyn and Bacon, Inc., 1962), p. 493.

CHAPTER VIII

The School as a Social System

The Organization

Formal. Waller focused attention upon the value of studying the school as a "social organism" whose unity derives from a definite population, a clearly defined political structure, a network of social relationships, and a culture of its own.[1] Since Waller, one of the major lines of investigation of the school has been its formal organization. This has been depicted as a hierarchy, at the top of which is the school board—a group of lay people who provide the link between school and community. Next come the ranks of administrators (superintendent, assistant superintendents, and principals). Then there are the teachers, the counsellors, and other members of the professional staff, as well as a group of nonprofessional people (bus drivers, custodians, and the like). Finally, there are the students, who form the broad base of the pyramid. Important problems are raised by such an authority structure for an institution the distinctive mission of which is education. The school board, for example, typically considers itself in an employer-employee, rather than client-professional, relationship with the other adult personnel of the school.[2] Administrative control over the whole range of school activities may conflict with the idea of teachers as professional people who are supposed to have "a high degree of autonomy over their own activities and considerable freedom in their decision-making."[3]

Informal. But the superordination-subordination pattern typical of the formal organization may be upset, or bypassed, on the

---

[1] Willard Waller, *The Sociology of Teaching* (New York: John Wiley & Sons, Inc., 1932), pp. 6–7.

[2] Wilbur B. Brookover, *A Sociology of Education* (New York: American Book Company, 1955), pp. 187–89.

[3] Neal Gross, "Sociology and the Study of Administration," in *The Social Sciences and Educational Administration,* edited by Lawrence M. Downey and Frederick Enns (Edmonton, Canada: The Division of Educational Administration, University of Alberta, 1963), p. 34.

basis of factors not shown on the organization chart. The teacher who is a lifelong resident of the community in which he teaches— who comes perhaps from a high-prestige family in that community —may well exert an influence that other teachers do not. Through long experience on the job, or a special position in the community, nonprofessional staff members may gain considerably more power than their subordinate position provides. A teacher in a school system studied by Iannacone[4] wielded greater power over policy-making than the principal of his school because he was a member of the executive board of the PTA, which—despite its semiformal status in the school system—had great prestige and authority. Another semiformal group—the Teachers' Association—provided a source of power that was used when the exclusively down-the-line communication characteristic of the formal system frustrated goals desired by teachers. This organization made possible a successful appeal beyond superintendent and school board to the community at large.

Iannacone protests, however, any absolute dichotomy between formal and informal organization and the tendency to conceive of the former as inherently restrictive and the latter as inherently liberating. Informal groups, he points out, can control, modify, even thwart the personal goals of the individual as much as formal organizations can, and he points to the function of a formal constitution in protecting individuals and minorities against arbitrary actions of informal groups. Organizational life is better conceptualized, he suggests, as a continuum, at the two poles of which are formal organization and pure friendship groups. Although it would seem wise for the administrator to study and take account of the shortcuts devised by the informal organization, revising the by-the-book procedures of the formal organization, not all customary behavior found in the informal systems is advantageous to the institution as a whole or to the people in it and, hence, should not be followed blindly. Congreve warns that the school is not a family, and that teachers do not expect the administration to satisfy their personal needs or to provide a great deal of personal attention; they prefer, rather,

> . . . the administrator who plans, organizes, and communicates in such ways as to insure that all are informed; that those affected

---

[4] D. E. Griffiths, *et al., Organizing Schools for Effective Education* (Danville, Ill.: Interstate Printers and Publishers, 1962), Part IV.

by pending changes are consulted; and that the professional needs prerequisite to effective teaching are satisfied.[5]

The administrator who becomes too involved in the highly personal interaction of the informal organization of his staff "may confuse satisfaction of individual needs with organizational goals, lose objectivity, and because he cannot interact at this level with all staff members, lose effective contact with many members of his staff."

Leadership Styles and Organizational Climates

"Democracy," "autocracy," and "laissez-faire." It was Waller's thesis that the school is typically organized on "some variant of the autocratic system," with power radiating from the top down. He claimed that this held true both for the relationships among the adults in the school and for the relationships between adults and students in the classroom. During the 1930's, educators of progressive persuasion launched a sharp attack upon authoritarian school administration on the grounds that the total school experience educates and that the child could scarcely learn "democracy" under teachers who were treated autocratically.

> Teachers will not facilitate freedom or growth on the part of pupils unless they themselves are given freedom by the administration. It is thus clear that there must be complete harmony between the philosophy of education which is basic to the school and the philosophy of leadership which is basic to the role of the teacher and the administrator.[6]

The progressive position appeared to receive "scientific" justification from the experiments of Lippitt and Lewin with small groups of eleven-year-old children who met after school to make masks, wood and soap carvings, and the like. An attempt was made to hold all factors constant in each group except the leadership roles—of which, by the time the experiments ended, there were three: democratic, autocratic, and laissez-faire.

Democratic and laissez-faire leadership differed from autocratic

[5] Willard J. Congreve, "Administrative Behavior and Staff Relations," *Administrator's Notebook*, VI, 2 (October 1957).

[6] Ernest O. Melby, "The Teacher and the School System," in *The Teacher and Society*, edited by William H. Kilpatrick (New York: Appleton-Century-Crofts, 1937), pp. 130–31.

leadership in that they left to the group control of the goals and the means of achieving the goals; the autocratic leader assumes control of goal and means himself. Democratic leadership differed from laissez-faire leadership in that it sought to stimulate group discussion and decision, while the laissez-faire leadership provided a minimum of help to the group.

The study appeared to show the advantages of democratic over the other two types of leadership. Although the quantity of work done under autocratic leadership was somewhat greater, work motivation and originality were stronger under democratic leadership; autocracy could create much hostility, aggression, and scapegoating, as well as discontent that did not appear on the surface; and there was more dependence and less individuality in autocracy, more group-mindedness and friendliness in democracy. Under laissez-faire, as compared with democratic leadership, there was less work accomplished, and poorer work, there was more play and at the same time more discontent expressed, and the boys expressed preference for their democratic leader.[7]

Effects on teachers and administrators.   Despite the distinction Lewin drew between laissez-faire and democratic leadership, *democratic* came to be identified with *permissiveness,* and a concern for human relations tended to replace an interest in the organization chart. Administrative theory today, however, recognizes both aspects of the organization: the formal role definitions determined by institutional requirements (in Getzel's terminology, the *nomothetic dimension*) and the personal needs of the individuals performing the roles (the *ideographic dimension*).[8] Accordingly, leadership is seen to involve both task-orientation or productivity, and group maintenance or morale functions; or what Halpin calls *initiating structure* and *consideration.*[9] Halpin defines the former as the leader's behavior in "delineating the relationship between himself and

---

[7] Kurt Lewin, Ronald Lippitt, and Ralph K. White, "Patterns of Aggressive Behavior in Experimentally Created 'Social Climates,' " *Journal of Social Psychology,* X (1939), 271–99; Ralph K. White and Ronald Lippitt, *Autocracy and Democracy* (New York: Harper & Row, Publishers, 1960), pp. 87–88.

[8] J. W. Getzels, "Administration as a Social Process," in *Administrative Theory in Education,* edited by A. W. Halpin (Chicago: Midwest Administration Center, 1958), Chap. 7; and J. W. Getzels and Egon C. Guba, "Social Behavior and the Administrative Process," *School Review,* XLV (Winter 1957), 423–41.

[9] A. W. Halpin, *Leadership Behavior of School Superintendents* (Chicago: Midwest Administration Center, 1956), p. 4.

members of the work group, and in endeavoring to establish well-defined patterns of organization, channels of communication, and methods of procedure," and the latter, as "behavior indicative of friendship, mutual trust, respect, and warmth in the relationship between the leader and members of his staff." He refuses to use the term *democratic leadership* because, applied in education, it has "immobilized more leaders than it has liberated" by convincing educational leaders that to take a stand is undemocratic. On Halpin's view, consideration—the equivalent of what *democratic* had come to mean—is a vital component of effective leadership, but it is not in opposition to the initiation of structure and, indeed, those superintendents who refuse to take a stand "eventually lose the respect of their staffs; teachers can quickly spot the phony who tries to hide his own ineptness in the soggy oatmeal of a pseudo group-process."[10]

Halpin's study of fifty Ohio superintendents showed that staff, school board, and teachers all agreed that ideal leadership involved both components, but that the behavior of the superintendents as described by the three groups fell significantly short of the ideal, primarily by failing to initiate structure to as great an extent as desirable, their strong point being high consideration for members of their staffs.[11]

In a later study of seventy-one elementary schools in six different regions of the United States, Halpin identified six kinds of "organizational climates," from "open" (flexible) to "closed" (rigid). A school's effectiveness was judged on the degree to which the principal was able to "create a 'climate' in which he, and other group members, can initiate and consummate acts of leadership"; a desirable organizational climate was assumed to be one in which leadership acts could emerge easily, from whatever source. What had earlier been called *initiation of structure* and *consideration* became the criterion of "thrust"—that is, leadership efforts to move the organization forward by setting an example of task-oriented behavior. Halpin saw "thrust," in turn, to reflect "authenticity": for the leader to take the risk of instituting change from a status satisfactory to the members of the group to a higher stage of organizational development demands that "the principal 'must stand for

---

[10] A. W. Halpin, "The Superintendent's Effectiveness as a Leader," *Administrator's Notebook,* VII, 2 (October 1958).

[11] Halpin, *Leadership Behavior of School Superintendents, op. cit.,* p. 70.

something,' " and let his teachers and the school's patrons know what he stands for. The concept of authenticity—not envisaged at the beginning of the study—emerged, for Halpin, as one of its most important concepts, in fact, as the key to understanding effective leadership among school executives. And he suggests a relationship between authenticity and the "marginal man," whose tendency to overconform, for the sake of acceptance by the group to which he aspires, causes him to deny something of himself, to become "inauthentic." Teaching, Halpin observes, is a "marginal profession," from the standpoint of salaries earned, lack of independence, the social mobility of teachers, and the fact that many teachers are "marginal students," drifting "down" from other curricula into teaching.[12]

Spindler's remarks on the "balancing" role of the school administrator—particularly the principal—are somewhat less harsh than Halpin's, for he points out that this role results from the fact that the school administrator "is caught squarely in the midst of the value conflicts that swirl around his position and the activity of the institution that he administers." Because he must maintain a working equilibrium of "at best antagonistically cooperative forces," and hence must "play his role to the satisfaction of many audiences simultaneously that are using different and potentially conflicting criteria of his performance," the school administrator is rarely an outspoken protagonist of a "consistent and vigorously profiled point of view."[13] Cornell found that teacher behavior may be influenced more by general organizational climate than by specific administrative actions. Teacher effectiveness, he observes, depended not upon the amount of participation of individual teachers in administrative policy-making but, rather, upon the "climate of the administrative environment in which participation takes place." More important than what a teacher actually does in sharing with the administration in the formation of policy is

1. The extent to which he expects he would be invited to share;
2. The extent to which he believes that the administration takes his invitation seriously enough to make it official (give responsibility);

---

[12] A. W. Halpin and Don B. Croft, *The Organizational Climate of Schools* (Chicago: Midwest Administration Center, 1963), pp. 8, 79.

[13] George D. Spindler, "The Role of the School Administrator," in *Education and Culture,* edited by George D. Spindler (New York: Holt, Rinehart & Winston, Inc., 1963), p. 238.

3. The extent that the administrator values the teacher participation enough that it bears influence on final decision.[14]

To use Halpin's term, what is important is how "authentic" democratic administration is.

Guba and Bidwell describe a "transactional" style of leadership that is more than a mean between nomothetic and ideographic leadership. Although the transactional leader both "sees the need for making clear the nature of the organizational roles and expectations" and also "attempts to structure institutional action so as to provide for individual fulfillment," he will shift the emphasis from the nomothetic to the ideographic as the situation demands; he "will attempt to assess each situation as it arises in terms of the extent to which nomothetic or ideographic responses are appropriate."[15] From the vantage point of 1960, White and Lippitt admit the oversimplifications that resulted from overgeneralizing the 1939 studies. The appeal of autocratic leadership, they point out, rests upon two legitimate facets of leadership: clarity of roles, and efficiency of group performance. They admit that members of a group may "cheerfully accept" many frustrations of personal needs if these are seen as means of accomplishing what the group wants to accomplish. But if goal accomplishment and clarity of roles are achieved in a democracy—and White and Lippitt assert they can be—democracy has a clear superiority, for the other major factors all favor democratic leadership: participation in group decisions is generally satisfying, a leader's consideration for the welfare of his followers is likely to be appreciated, and freedom (at least freedom from needless and irrational restrictions, and particularly freedom of communication upward in the power hierarchy) is normally desired. In short, White and Lippitt reassert the difference between laissez-faire and democratic leadership, describing the latter as closer to what Gibbs calls *variable leadership technique*—that is, a leadership that is "adapted to all the elements of the situation."[16]

---

[14] Francis G. Cornell, "When Should Teachers Share in Making Administrative Decisions?" *Nation's Schools,* V (May 1954), 43–45. Reprinted, with permission, from *The Nation's Schools,* May 1954. Copyright © 1954, The Modern Hospital Publishing Co., Inc., Chicago. All rights reserved.

[15] Egon G. Guba and C. E. Bidwell, *Administrative Relationships* (Chicago: Midwest Administration Center, 1957), p. 11.

[16] Cecil Gibbs, "Leadership," in *Handbook of Social Psychology,* edited by Gardner Lindzey (Reading, Mass.: Addison-Wesley Publishing Company, Inc. 1954), Vol. II, p. 911.

Leadership Behavior in the Classroom

Expected teacher roles. Research into leadership styles of teachers in the classroom has utilized categories paralleling those employed in studies of leadership in the adult organization. Following Waller, Brookover observes that teachers are expected to maintain dominance, social distance, and respect; although where Waller accounts for this as necessary to overcome "resistance to learning," Brookover refers to the support this role receives from folk tales, cartoons, and literature, and to the expectations of adults, who regard the ability to maintain discipline as the first requirement of the successful teacher.[17] A combination of small-group research, the mental hygiene movement, counselling theory, and progressive education philosophy, resulted in a "democratic" definition of the teacher's classroom role. At the college level, a number of studies, expertly summarized by Anderson,[18] opposed the lecture and discussion methods, or instructor-centered and student-centered teaching.[19] As in the case of the adult organization, the relationships between leadership style, effectiveness, and satisfaction in the classroom were found to be far from simple, as evidenced by contradictory results obtained by various studies. Brookover, for example, found a negative relationship between student-teacher congeniality (democratic leadership) and amount of American history learned, leading him to conclude that students seem to learn more from the more authoritarian teachers, although they apparently like the friendly teachers more.[20] In explaining his findings, which he conceded contradicted both the results of other studies and "common sense," Brookover turned to the "traditional patterns of expectancy" of students for teacher domination, so that permissive teaching was taken to imply that learning was not desired. The contradictory results of college studies have caused Anderson, like Halpin, to conclude that "the authoritarian-democratic construct, as far as education is concerned at least, has far outlived its usefulness either

---

[17] Brookover, *op. cit.*, pp. 232–35; see also Waller, *op. cit.*, pp. 8, 195–96.

[18] Richard C. Anderson, "Learning in Discussion: A Résumé of Authoritarian-Democratic Studies," *Harvard Educational Review*, XXIX (Summer 1959), 201–15.

[19] Lauren G. Wispe, "Teaching Methods Research," *The American Psychologist*, VIII (April 1953), 147–50.

[20] Wilbur B. Brookover, "The Social Roles of Teachers and Pupil Achievement," *American Sociological Review*, VIII (August 1943), 389–93.

as a guide to research or as an interpretation of leadership behavior."

Effect on student needs. Wispe, however, observes that, despite the emphasis of the student-centered orientation upon the importance of student personality development, research has evidenced little concern for the effect of different teaching methods upon different patterns of student needs. A study that investigated these relationships discovered that students with high needs for structure were extremely critical of permissive classes and instructors, and, similarly, those with high autonomy needs were critical of the "directive" classroom.[21] According to Riessman, the progressive approach, despite its emphasis on learning by doing, fails with the culturally deprived child, whose cognitive style demands structure.[22] In general, as White and Lippitt have agreed, when the learning situation is such as to demand task-orientation—when passing an examination is at stake, for example—students will be frustrated by permissive leadership; " 'progressive education' is not necessarily what the students themselves want."[23]

Brim points out that the classroom group, like all groups, has two general kinds of needs: "instrumental" and "expressive." The relationship of these to initiation of structure and consideration is clear; but, unlike Halpin, Brim believes these to be relatively incompatible roles which, in fact, are taken by different people in informal groups. The problem of the teacher, as the sole leader in the classroom, involves handling both roles. Brim concludes that the studies show the dominant role for teachers is task-oriented ("instrumental"); that the teacher accepts this role at the expense of "expressive" or morale considerations, gaining respect but losing attractiveness in doing so. Both students and teachers wish more attention could be given the expressive role, but when this happens, learning suffers. As a consequence, the teacher faces contradictory demands in the classroom.[24]

---

[21] See Lauren G. Wispe, "Evaluating Section Teaching Methods in the Introductory Course," *Journal of Educational Research*, XLV (1951), 161–86; especially the section, "The Reactions of Three Student Response Groups to Directive and Permissive Teaching," pp. 171–77.

[22] Frank Reissman, *The Culturally Deprived Child* (New York: Harper & Row, Publishers), p. 72.

[23] White and Lippitt, *op. cit.*, pp. 261–62.

[24] Orville G. Brim, Jr., *Sociology and the Field of Education* (New York: Russell Sage Foundation, 1958), p. 49.

The Student in the Social System
of the School

Status. Students, from the standpoint of the total school hierarchy, are at the bottom of the pyramid, yet exhibit differences in
status. In early studies, such as *Elmtown's Youth,* student status was
viewed as a direct reflection of the social position of the student's
family. Dissatisfied with the social class hypothesis, Gordon[25] focused on the internal social system of a Midwestern suburban high
school, and explained the behavior of adolescents by reference to
their desire to achieve a "general social status" within the organization of the school. Opportunity for status achievement was available in three spheres: (1) the formal organization of the school
which prescribed learning achievement; (2) the system of student
organizations (extracurricular activities); and (3) small friendship
cliques. Gordon concluded that the primary means for defining social status was the system of student organizations; achievement in
the formal organization of the school, as measured by grades earned,
was least significantly related to general status.

The peer group. Recognition of the importance of the peer
group—Coleman's "adolescent society"—has resulted in a number
of studies of its impact on the educative process. The peer group
has been shown to exert some influence on the retention of students
in school, directly by the extent of participation in school activities
and indirectly by the effect of participation upon learning. Hollingshead reported that "peer-group isolation" was given by Elmtown
dropouts as one of the reasons for leaving school. Gordon found
that about one fifth of all students in Wabash High School took no
part in organized activities, and an additional one fifth participated
very little, resulting in "a type of social interaction among persons
variously placed on the status continuum whose relationships increasingly are characterized by social distance, differential association, and absence of communication."[26] If Taba is right, inability
(for economic or personality reasons) to conform to dress, dating,
and other requirements set by the "elite" groups affects school
achievement:

---

[25] C. Wayne Gordon, *The Social System of the High School* (New York: The
Macmillan Company, 1957).

[26] *Ibid.,* p. 77.

. . . the lack of sense of belonging affects self-expectations and motivation regarding academic success, and therefore also academic achievement, because integration of individuals in school groups seems to enhance motivation for learning, while disintegration, cleavage, and isolation lessen effort and motivation.[27]

Tyler notes the influence of the peer group on student choice of subject-matter fields and courses. The image the peer group holds of a liberal arts student compared with its image of a home economics major, for example, may encourage a student to enroll in one area rather than another without reference to his own special abilities and interest in the field, the quality of faculty and facilities, or the economic opportunities it offers for the future. Differences in attitudes of peer groups in urban and rural environments toward the college preparatory curriculum, and of girls and boys toward mathematics and the sciences as compared with the humanities, also may result in a "failure to actualize human potential."[28]

As in factories, where work groups set norms which they consider reasonable and which they defend against efforts of management to increase production beyond these norms, so may student groups set work standards. The ways in which medical students decide on what they wish to learn, what and how they ought to study, and the shortcuts they devise more or less in defiance of faculty instruction, are described in detail by Hughes, Becker, and Geer,[29] who found the student culture to be both "an accommodation on the part of the students to the facts of life of the school" and "a mechanism that creates the conditions for considerable deviance from formally stated institutional roles." According to Rossi, a large part of student underachievement in college results from the informal pressures of the groups into which students form themselves—an underachievement he believes to be particularly chronic among the more advantaged college students who come from the private preparatory schools

[27] Hilda Taba, *School Culture, Studies of Participation and Leadership* (Washington, D.C.: American Council on Education, 1955), pp. 114–15. By permission of the National Conference of Christians and Jews.

[28] Ralph Tyler, "The Impact of Students on Schools and Colleges," in *Social Forces Influencing American Education,* edited by Nelson B. Henry, Sixtieth Yearbook of the National Society for The Study of Education (Chicago: The University of Chicago Press, 1961), pp. 171–81.

[29] Everett C. Hughes, Howard S. Becker, and Blanche Geer, "Student Culture and Academic Effort," in *The American College,* edited by Nevitt Sanford (New York: John Wiley & Sons, Inc., 1962), pp. 521–58.

and among students attending the more prominent undergraduate colleges.[30]

The emphasis on athletics.   The central importance of athletics in the high school culture, and the undervaluing of the brilliant student by high school students as a group—and even more so by their elites—have been stressed by Gordon, Coleman, and Tannenbaum.[31] This has influenced even the high-ability students, according to Coleman, who marshals evidence to show that the high school students who are considered "the intellectuals," and who consider themselves such, "are not really those of highest intelligence, but are only the ones who are willing to work hard at a relatively unrewarded activity." Coleman concluded that there is "something about the high school itself, rather invariant from school to school, which creates a strong bias toward athletes and athletics," a bias he attributed to the presence of interscholastic athletic competition. The athlete gains status because he is "doing something for the school and community in leading his team to victory, for it is a school victory." The successes of the outstanding student, on the other hand, are not only purely personal, but often they are at the expense of his peers, who must work harder to keep up with him. This shows, according to Coleman,

> . . . the effects of the structure of activities on the status system, and as a consequence, on the allocation of energies in scholastic directions. School forces a scholar to choose between being *selfish* by studying hard, and being *unselfish* by working for the glory of the school in its interscholastic games.[32]

Coleman proposed, therefore, the substitution of interscholastic and intramural competition for the present interpersonal competition for grades, so that scholarly activity would receive the kind of reinforcement from community and fellow students now bestowed upon athletics. Such a choice, he admitted, would demand the inventiveness to create intellectual games (such as the "political games" developed by Rand Corporation, or the "management games" used in training business executives), group problems and projects in science, and

[30] Cited by Tyler, *op. cit.,* p. 176.

[31] Abraham J. Tannenbaum, "Adolescent's Attitudes Toward Academic Brilliance," unpublished doctoral Dissertation, presented at Columbia University, New York, N.Y., 1960.

[32] Reprinted with permission of The Free Press of Glencoe from *The Adolescent Society* by James S. Coleman, pp. 133, 265, 309, 310. Copyright © 1961 by The Free Press, a Corporation.

the like, for such competition; an extension, in short, of the principle embodied in present debate teams, music and drama contests, and mathematics tournaments. Such tactics, which would seek to use informal group rewards to further intellectual activity rather than to fight their influence, would involve difficulties—less evaluation of individual achievement, for example. But, Coleman thinks, they would be more practical than the attempt to counter prevailing social trends.

The responsibility of society.   Such an approach raises serious problems concerning the responsibility of adults, both within and outside the school, for the structure of activities in the school. Friedenberg believes that Coleman makes a better case for the isolation of the adolescent society than for its triviality, and maintains that both characteristics are "largely responses to the greater triviality and corruption of much of our adult society." Coleman's findings are "more a credit to the adolescent society than an indictment of it," for "it is the level and conception of scholarship the youngsters have actually experienced in the high school as it now is that have led them to rate it way below athletics." Sports are "at least real and manly," and demand "true competences" in contrast to the "phony scholarship" of the school: the "magnificent" appearance of boys who have just won a basketball tournament from a major city high school may be contrasted with the "sheepishness" which they must display upon emerging from a "Problems of Democracy" class in their small, segregated Louisiana high school.[33]

Both Friedenberg and Coleman criticize the character of intellectual activities provided by the high school, referring to the evidence supplied by creativity studies that teachers prefer conventional rather than creative manifestations of ability on the part of students. Coleman employs the values of the larger society, however, to explain the "puzzle of Executive Heights," the school in which students individually were very interested in the good grades necessary for admission to "good" colleges, but whose "leading crowd" was even less oriented toward the "brilliant-student" image than the elites of other schools. Here, the girls felt less than did the girls of the other nine schools Coleman studied that good grades contrib-

---

[33] Edgar Z. Friedenberg, "Hot Rods and Questionnaires," *Commentary*, XXXII, 5 (November 1961), 445–47. Copyright © American Jewish Committee. Reprinted by permission of *Commentary* and the author.

uted to their popularity with boys. Coleman associates these results with the concern of upper-middle-class parents in the cities with the social skills and self-assurance of their children, a consequent liberation from parental control, and a corresponding emphasis by the adolescents on those areas in which they have "responsibility and authority to act: the social games of dating and parties, athletic contests for the boys, yearbook, newspaper, and drama group for the girls." Good grades, on the other hand, represent "acquiescence and conformity to adult constraints," and those girls who seek them are not popular with middle-class boys. That the Executive Heights girls were by far the highest in the proportion choosing the "leader in activities" image Coleman takes to indicate that as society becomes more and more white-collar, the kind of image that girls will be strong for in school will be only "obliquely" related to intellectual achievement, and will be more nearly "the teen-age replica of the adult clubwoman."[34]

As a result of her study of extracurricular programs in seven types of schools in different regions of the United States, Hilda Taba, however, placed responsibility squarely upon the school's lack of conscious rationale for extracurricular activities.[35] In the programs she studied, Taba found that typically only about half the school's population was involved, "usually the half that least needed what such participation had to offer." In part, this was because schools use participation in extracurricular activities as a means of rewarding achievement elsewhere, rather than to "provide training in social association, in skills of leadership, or in group participation to all who need such training." Membership in organizations "established to reinforce the teaching of democracy" frequently is "subverted into a reward for academic proficiency, a matter of social prestige, or a protection for social exclusiveness." Typically, Taba found, the programs enhance rather than minimize egocentric strivings and individual popularity by channeling leadership to a few students and adults. Students learn "verbal allegiance to democratic values while practicing habits of authoritarian control, social indifference, and dishonesty of group purposes." Above all, these school programs "tended to reflect the pressures, biases, emphases,

---

[34] Coleman, *op. cit.*, pp. 292, 259.
[35] Taba, *op. cit.*, pp. 115–17.

and prejudices of the surrounding environment, instead of consciously supplementing gaps in them or correcting their flaws."

Cultural influences. Havighurst has declared education to be more responsive to than responsible for social forces. The difficulties involved in arguing for either the autonomy or the impotence of the schools in creating a better society have emerged clearly in debates on this issue since the 1930's. Theodore Brameld and Robert M. Hutchins, although at opposite ends of the philosophical spectrum, appear to agree in attributing to the schools a relatively autonomous status. But although Brameld continues the social reconstructionist views of Counts and Rugg, he does so with a clear recognition of the "powerful resistances to consciously directed change that are typical of cultures."[36] Although Hutchins has advocated the establishment of educational ends and means upon an Aristotelian metaphysics of human nature, declaring, therefore, that "education should be everywhere the same," he also has said that "whatever is wrong with education" comes down to "what is wrong with the country" for the educational system will always cultivate "whatever is honored in a country."[37]

To accept the premise that the school can only reflect the culture, however, may lead to serious difficulties, both practical and theoretical. Callahan's study of the adoption of the business ideology in educational administration[38] depicts in painful detail the vulgarities resulting from a capitulation to the idea that education is a business and the school a factory. Conant sought to defend the public schools by reminding their critics that "education is a social process." As a consequence, before judging a school we must

> . . . analyze the families from which it draws its students and the opportunities presented to its graduates. What may be a satisfactory curriculum for one group of pupils may be highly unsatisfactory for another. And the difference is often due not to discrepancies in the intellectual capacities of the students but to the social situation in which the boys and girls are placed. This in turn depends on the

---

[36] Theodore Brameld, "The Meeting of Educational and Anthropological Theory," in *Education and Anthropology,* George D. Spindler, ed. (Stanford: Stanford University Press, 1955), p. 223.

[37] Robert Maynard Hutchins, *The Higher Learning in America* (New Haven: Yale University Press, 1936), p. 66; *Education for Freedom* (Baton Rouge, La.: Louisiana State University Press, 1947), pp. 48–49.

[38] Raymond E. Callahan, *The Cult of Efficiency* (Chicago: The University of Chicago Press, 1962).

nature of the local community of which the pupils and their parents are a part. To be specific, the problems facing the principals of three high schools—one in an industrialized section of a congested steel town, another in a rural area in the Middle West, a third in a well-to-do suburb of Chicago, St. Louis, or New York—are totally different. In the first two cases, for example, only a very small fraction of the graduates of the schools will expect to continue formal education; in the third instance practically all the pupils and their parents will expect the schools to prepare them for admittance to a college or university.[38]

So bald an endorsement of social determinism made Conant himself uneasy. Declaring it possible to "combine the analytic approach of the sociologist and anthropologist with a firm belief in standards," he expressed the hope that the public schools would be pervaded by the point of view of a "tough-minded idealist," leaning heavily, on the one side, toward "a certain type of social science" but, on the other, being "almost fanatically humanitarian, tolerant, and individualistic." He advocated enough "American idealism in the mixture to insure against any disguised Toryism gaining the upper hand" but "enough tough-minded critical quality also to prevent the planning of Utopias from usurping all the energies of our educators."

In fact, the determinist interpretation of the school tends to demand too little of educators; the conception of the school as an autonomous agency tends to demand too much. Caution in urging the school to undertake the responsibility for social reform without due consideration of its social basis may be one of the fruits of understanding education as a social process. This cannot, however, relieve educators of the responsibility of thinking, on an operational level, about the implications of social and ethical ideals for education, and of allying the school with those forces which work to bring a society more closely in accord with those ideals.

---

[38] James B. Conant, *Education in a Divided World* (Cambridge, Mass.: Harvard University Press, 1948), pp. 48, 51–52.

Bibliography

Anderson, Archibald, *et al., The Theoretical Foundations of Education.* Urbana, Illinois: Bureau of Research and Service, College of Education, University of Illinois, 1951.

Borrowman, Merle, *The Liberal and Technical in Teacher Education.* New York: Teachers College, Bureau of Publications, Columbia University, 1956.

Brameld, Theodore, *Cultural Foundations of Education.* New York: Harper & Row, Publishers, 1957.

Brauner, Charles J., *American Educational Theory.* Englewood Cliffs, N.J.: Prentice-Hall, Inc., 1964.

Brim, Orville G., Jr., *Sociology and the Field of Education.* New York: Russell Sage Foundation, 1958.

Brookover, Wilbur B., *A Sociology of Education,* 2nd ed. (with David Gottlieb). New York: American Book Company, 1964.

Butts, R. Freeman, and Lawrence A. Cremin, *A History of Education in American Culture.* New York: Holt, Rinehart & Winston, Inc., 1953.

Charters, W. W., Jr., and N. L. Gage, *Readings in the Social Psychology of Education.* Boston: Allyn and Bacon, 1963.

Cremin, Lawrence A., *The Transformation of the School.* New York: Alfred A. Knopf, Inc., 1962.

Cremin, Lawrence A. (ed.), *The Republic and the School, Horace Mann on the Education of Free Men.* New York: Teachers College, Bureau of Publications, Columbia University, Classics in Education No. 1, 1957.

Curti, Merle, *The Social Ideas of American Educators.* Paterson, N.J.: Pageant Books, Inc., 1959.

Dahlke, H. Otto, *Values in Culture and Classroom.* New York: Harper & Row, Publishers, 1958.

Dworkin, Martin S. (ed.), *Dewey on Education.* New York: Teachers College, Bureau of Publications, Columbia University, Classics in Education No. 3, 1959.

Edward, Newton, and Herman G. Richey, *The School in the American Social Order.* New York: McGraw-Hill Book Company, 1964.

Gage, N. L. (ed.), *Handbook of Research on Teaching.* Chicago: Rand McNally & Co., 1963.

Graham, Grace, *The Public School in the American Community.* New York: Harper & Row, Publishers, 1963.

Grambs, Jean D., and L. Morris McLure, *Foundations of Teaching.* New York: Holt, Rinehart & Winston, Inc., 1964.

Gross, Richard E. (ed.), *Heritage of American Education.* Boston: Allyn and Bacon, Inc., 1962.

Henry, Nelson B. (ed.), *Social Forces Affecting American Education,* Sixtieth Yearbook of the National Society for the Study of Education. Chicago: University of Chicago Press, 1961.

Hodgkinson, Harold L., *Education in Social and Cultural Perspectives.* Englewood Cliffs, N.J.: Prentice-Hall, Inc., 1962.

Kallenbach, Warren, and Harold M. Hodges, Jr., *Education and Society.* Columbus, Ohio: Charles E. Merrill Books, Inc., 1963.

Kimball, Solon T., and James E. McClelland, Jr., *Education and the New America.* New York: Random House, 1962.

Kneller, George F. (ed.), *Foundations of Education.* New York: John Wiley & Sons, Inc., 1963.

Mercer, Blaine W., and Edwin R. Carr, *Education and the Social Order.* New York: Holt, Rinehart & Winston, Inc., 1957.

Olsen, Edward G. (ed.), *The School and Community Reader.* New York: The Macmillan Company, 1963.

Rugg, Harold (ed.), *Readings in the Foundations of Education.* New York: Teachers College, Bureau of Publications, Columbia University, 1941.

Rugg, Harold, *The Teacher of Teachers.* New York: Harper & Row, Publishers, 1952.

Sanford, Nevitt (ed.), *The American College.* New York: John Wiley & Sons, Inc., 1962.

Spindler, George D. (ed.), *Education and Culture.* New York: Holt, Rinehart & Winston, Inc., 1963.

Stanley, William O., *et al., Social Foundations of Education.* New York: Holt, Rinehart & Winston, Inc., 1956.

Stiles, Lindley J., *The Teacher's Role in American Society.* New York: Harper & Row, Publishers, Fourteenth Yearbook of the John Dewey Society, 1957.

Thayer, V. T., *The Role of the School in American Society.* New York: Dodd Mead & Co., 1961.

Waller, Willard, *The Sociology of Teaching.* New York: John Wiley & Sons, Inc., 1932.

Warner, W. Lloyd, Robert J. Havighurst, and Martin Loeb, *Who Shall Be Educated?* New York: Harper & Row, Publishers, 1944.

Weiss, Thomas M., and Kenneth B. Hoover, *Scientific Foundations of Education.* Dubuque, Iowa: William C. Brown Co., Publishers, 1964.

Index

115